THE BOY IN THE WOODS

THE BOY IN THE WOODS

A TRUE STORY OF SURVIVAL DURING THE SECOND WORLD WAR

MAXWELL SMART

HarperCollinsPublishersLtd

HarperCollins books may be purchased for educational, business or sales promotional use
through our Special Markets Department.

HarperCollins Publishers Ltd
Bay Adelaide Centre, East Tower
22 Adelaide Street West, 41st Floor
Toronto, Ontario, Canada
M5H 4E3

www.harpercollins.ca

Library and Archives Canada Cataloguing in Publication

Title: The boy in the woods / Maxwell Smart. | Other titles: Chaos to canvas
Names: Smart, Maxwell, 1930- author.
Description: Previously published under title: Chaos to canvas. Published by: Toronto :
The Azrieli Foundation, 2018. | Includes bibliographical references and index.
Identifiers: Canadiana (print) 20220143463 | Canadiana (ebook) 2022014348X
ISBN 9781443466424 (softcover) | ISBN 9781443466431 (ebook)
Subjects: LCSH: Smart, Maxwell, 1930- | LCSH: Holocaust, Jewish (1939-1945)—Poland—
Personal narratives. | LCSH: Holocaust survivors—Canada—Biography. | LCSH: Polish people—
Canada—Biography. | CSH: Polish Canadians—Biography. | LCGFT: Autobiographies.
Classification: LCC DS134.72.S63 A3 2022 | DDC 940.53/18092—dc23

Printed and bound in the United States of America
LSC/C 9 8 7 6 5 4 3 2 1

CONTENTS

ABOUT THE GLOSSARY

The following memoir contains a number of terms, concepts and historical references that may be unfamiliar to the reader. For information on major organizations; significant historical events and people; geographical locations; religious and cultural terms; and foreign-language words and expressions that will help give context and background to the events described in the text, please see the glossary beginning on page 181.

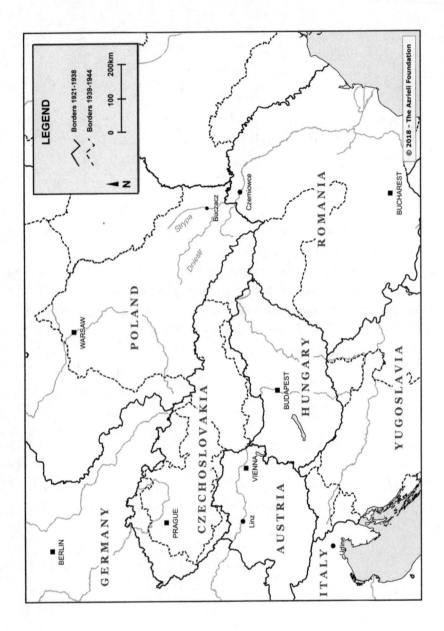

GERMANY

BERLIN

POLAND

WARSAW

Strypa

Dniestr

Buczacz

Czerniowce

CZECHOSLOVAKIA

PRAGUE

ROMANIA

BUCHAREST

HUNGARY

BUDAPEST

VIENNA

Linz

AUSTRIA

YUGOSLAVIA

ITALY

Udine

This book is dedicated to the memory of my parents, Faigie and Lieb Fromm; my sister, Zonia; and all sixty-two members of my extended family who perished in the Holocaust.

To my beloved late wife, Helen Safran Smart.

To my beloved wife, Tina Russo Smart, without whose encouragement and patience this book would not be possible.

To my children, Faigie, Lorne and Anthony.

To my grandchildren, Tara, Jay, Brandon and Adam.

I would like to make a special dedication to a poor Polish farmer named Jasko Rudnicki. He risked his life and that of his wife, Kasia, and their two children, while sharing what little he had with me. He saved my life when I hid from the Nazis and their Ukrainian collaborators during the Holocaust.

Thank you, Jasko and Kasia, for giving me my life.

A special dedication in memory of my best friend, Janek, without whom I never would have survived in the woods.

ACKNOWLEDGEMENTS

I never thought that the story of my life would make it to the printed page. For this, I have a number of people to thank. It is largely because of my wife, Tina, and my son Anthony that this book was written. Tina started questioning me about my past, and I felt comfortable talking openly with her. She told me that I should not be ashamed of my suffering and urged me to write my story, to record everything that I could recall, and to tell the story to my children and grandchildren because they had no idea how I had survived. Without this story, they wouldn't know who I am and where I come from. Tina believed that such a project would resolve the many conflicted feelings that I have about being a child survivor of the Holocaust.

I enlisted a friend of mine, Joe King, to help me research the historical details in this book. Meetings were arranged between me, Joe, Tina and Anthony, and most of our weekends over the course of two years were spent writing this book. It was a long, tedious, stressful and depressing journey, and it resulted in many painful memories. Often, after a session, I would be in a morose mood for days. With the help of Anthony, Joe and Tina, I feel that I have accomplished something important: I have written my book.

I wish to extend my deep appreciation to my loving wife, Tina, who has encouraged me and assisted me in writing this book.

I must particularly acknowledge the immense services provided by Anthony Katsoudas in preparing the manuscript. He worked intensely and tirelessly, prodding me ("Daddy" to him) to tell my story and then laboriously transcribing three hundred pages of notes. There would have been no book without this scholarly effort by Anthony, who was determined to see my story become a reality.

A special thanks to my daughter, Faigie, who spent hours and hours editing my story. I also thank my son Lorne for his encouragement.

I would also like to thank the late Joe King, whose experience in research journalism made this book possible. He was a historian and author of four other books. The many meetings and discussions we had in my home every Sunday for two years were essential in piecing together my story. Heather Solomon-Bowden, an award-winning arts journalist and copy editor, also helped me. I also thank Susan Cushway for all her years of work and for her help with typing my memoirs; we are proud to call her our adopted family.

I am most grateful for the assistance provided by Janice Rosen and Helene Valle from the Canadian Jewish Congress National Archives, Carrie-Ann Smith from the Pier 21 Archives in Halifax, Public Archives of Canada and Bibliothèque Nationale du Québec.

Much gratitude to Zbigniew (Joseph) Smigowski, my most dedicated right-hand man for 40 years.

Thank you Melissa Mikel for your hard work on this project.

I want to express my deepest appreciation and gratitude to the Azrieli Foundation and my heartfelt gratitude to all their dedicated staff, especially Jody Spiegel, Arielle Berger and Elin Beaumont.

I would never believe this was possible without the effort of Saloon Media director Rebecca Snow, producer Steve Gamaster and their incredible and talented crew.

Thank you all from the bottom of my heart. I'm grateful to everyone who has contributed to finding Janek's family and Tova. You all gave me the coda to my life.

Lastly, I acknowledge information obtained from the following publications:

Trudy Duivenvoorden Mitic and J.P. LeBlanc, *Pier 21: The Gateway that Changed Canada* (Lancelot Press, 1988); Ben Lappin, *The Redeemed Children: The Story of the Rescue of War Orphans by the Jewish Community of Canada* (University of Toronto Press, 1963); Fraidie Martz, *Open Your Hearts: The Story of the Jewish War Orphans in Canada* (Véhicule Press, 1996).

FOREWORD

This is a story of courage and survival. Millions perished in the Holocaust — often helpless to save themselves in the face of the incredible brutality of the Nazis and their numerous collaborators. Here we have the memoir of a little boy who is about to be forced onto a truck, en route to his execution. The mother cries out to her little boy, "Save yourself!"— and he bravely defies the odds and lives.

This dramatic story unfolds in a small town in Poland — Buczacz — now part of Ukraine, where thousands of collaborators turned on their Jewish neighbours, killing them and looting whatever they could. When the war shuddered to its bloody finale, only one hundred of about eight thousand Jews in the town had survived. Maxwell Smart was one of them.

In rags, starving, narrowly and repeatedly escaping death at the hands of the Nazis and Ukrainians, Maxwell — although only a boy at the time — displays a remarkable blend of courage, compassion and maturity.

An orphan, he makes his way to Canada — a country that, prior to and during the war, had turned its back on endangered Jews who sought refuge. The countries wise enough to provide a home for the refugees were enriched by their newcomers' extraordinary contributions. Canada stood at the bottom of the ladder in terms of saving these imperilled people. Only after the true horror of the Holocaust was revealed did Canada's leaders (and not all of them) liberalize their immigration policies.

Thousands of survivors living in Montreal have never told their stories. The voices of Maxwell Smart and others must be heard, as we still encounter people who downplay or even dismiss the largest and most documented mass murder in human history. Regrettably, there are no words to convey the full horror of the Holocaust. Only the individual experiences of people like Maxwell Smart, painfully recalled, begin to describe the monumental crimes of the Nazi Party and its collaborators.

And from the brutality of war has emerged a celebrated artist offering the world, in sharp contrast, beautiful images. Maxwell Smart describes himself as an abstract expressionist — that is, he belongs to a school of artists born in the wake of World War II. Yet Maxwell's paintings are marked by a difference in style and content — his paintings are enriched by his past. In many ways, they are subconscious creations, digging deep into hidden memories of flight and fear and fantasy. One cannot be untouched after living in constant danger for years, detached from virtually all human contact and seeking distraction from gnawing hunger. These are the elements that make Maxwell's canvases dynamic and different. The forests in which he hid, the planets and stars distracting him from his endlessly endangered existence, and even the moments of serenity, are all reflected in his work.

Furthermore, he paints enormous pieces. This is not the work of someone seeking to produce an oeuvre easily and without pain. Many paintings are so big that they are suitable only for a gallery, an institution or a mansion. Paintings by Maxwell Smart hang in various galleries and collections. In 2006, the opening of the gallery bearing his name saw hundreds of people come to pay tribute — and to buy paintings.

Art columnist Heather Solomon, who has written about Montreal artists for more than twenty years, labelled Maxwell Smart "the jewel of the Montreal art scene." I was present when Solomon first encountered Maxwell's work in his St. Laurent, Quebec, gallery. She entered the gallery and was immediately drawn to closely examine a painting of stars. This is how Heather described the moment: "Through a door, the ceiling swoops upward to eighteen feet and your eyes widen with the rush of colour and energy emanating from large-scale paintings that practically sing with life."[1]

Among those paying tribute to Maxwell at his gallery opening was accomplished Canadian artist Sydney Berne. Berne was impressed by what he called Max's "unflagging optimism," declaring, "Having experienced childhood misery in darkness, as he hid from the Nazis, he now revels in light with his exuberant will to live and to paint."[2]

For the seven-year-old boy who was thrilled by his teacher's encouraging words about his art seven decades ago, in another world, life has come full circle — and he has joyfully learned the truth in Franz Kafka's statement that "anyone who keeps the ability to see beauty never grows old."

Joe King (1923–2013)
Montreal, Quebec

---

1 Heather Solomon, "Second career flowers for Maxwell Smart," *Canadian Jewish News*, September 14, 2006.
2 Naomi Gold, "Into the Light … the Art of (Being) Maxwell Smart," www.jewish directories.com, 2006.

AUTHOR'S PREFACE

You might think that I was one of the lucky ones — a young Jewish boy living in Poland during World War II who never saw the inside of a concentration camp. But my memories of those long days and longer nights when, from the age of twelve, I found myself completely alone bring back the uncontrollable panic and dread of being discovered in my hiding place, the hunger of my starving body and the absolute fear that everyone was my enemy. The severe, painful cold of the winter months are part of me every day and night, even now, more than seven decades later.

For a large portion of the last seventy years, I attempted to block out the terrifying, psychologically and physically scarring nightmare of what happened to my family and me during World War II and the German occupation of Poland. Understandably, I did not want to remember or relive the past, and so attempted to erase this tragic period of my life and tried to pretend that it never happened. With much determination, I was able to create a new life for myself in Montreal and lock away my painful past. In essence, my new life started when I arrived in Canada — or so I tried to convince myself. I desperately did not want to remember those horrible Holocaust years, and when for a moment a memory would intrude on the present, I would become depressed for days. I would get angry and anxious and ask myself, Is this normal? Am I normal?

The horrors of the Holocaust were not discussed and not even fully acknowledged by many in the Jewish community in Montreal after the war, and many Canadian Jews were not really interested in the subject. It seemed they felt dissociated from it, and they appeared to be more concerned about the fact that newcomers were taking away their jobs. When I first arrived in Canada, many people would ask where I was from, and they would question me about my city, but they never asked about my parents or family or what I had experienced or how I survived the inconceivable savagery. They seemed disinterested in the barbarity that was experienced by a twelve-year-old boy, a homeless orphan who survived the war by stealing and begging for food, who risked his life every day in a desperate hunt for something to eat, who could easily have been shot to death for simply scrounging for food — just because he was a Jew.

In my case, I was extremely lucky to have the help of Jasko Rudnicki, a very poor Polish farmer with a heart of gold. During the long period in which I meticulously reviewed the painful memories of my perilous existence, I realized that Jasko had repeatedly saved my life. My aunt and uncle had made an arrangement to provide him with money periodically — a small amount that was necessary for the farmer, who lived a marginal existence, to assist me. When the funds stopped arriving after the second payment, he still continued to help me, for about two years.

In May 2008, during a visit to the Yad Vashem Holocaust Remembrance Center in Jerusalem, I made a formal submission recommending that Jasko Rudnicki be honoured with the title "Righteous Among the Nations." In spite of the Germans' threat that they would kill anyone who aided Jews, there are more than twenty thousand non-Jews who have been designated as "Righteous Among the Nations" by Yad Vashem. This figure may represent only a fraction of those who risked everything to help their neighbours. The process for verifying the contributions made on behalf of a nominee require at least two eyewitnesses, and in many instances, no one survived to verify what happened. Although I survived much of the war as a result of Jasko's generosity and compassion, unfortunately I had no documents to prove how he had helped me, and I had no way of finding any of his descendants who could confirm the story. I do still hope to find them one day, and formally recognize Jasko and Kasia's selflessness. I know without a doubt that I never could have survived if not for their care.

A Canadian Jew who lived in peace, with a family, a home and children, and who was never hungry, could never fully understand how I survived. Today, at the age of eighty-five, while I write this book and analyze the many encounters that I had with death, I still try to understand how I survived so much hardship, pain and brutality. Was there a reason that I was chosen to survive?

I could easily have been caught and killed at any point throughout my years in hiding. The vast number of Jews who encountered even one of the many situations I was in did not survive. Because of this, I believe that it was a miracle that I was spared death. There is no logical or rational way to otherwise describe my survival. While reading this book, you will realize that sometimes miracles do happen, because they happened to me.

After all this, I made a life for myself in Canada, and even when I got married I never discussed my past. But life doesn't follow a plan or unfold in the way you think it should. Unexpected things happened, like the death of my wife, Helen, my love, a beautiful fifty-two-year-old woman who became ill with cancer and passed away quickly. All of a sudden I was a fifty-five-year-old man, alone. That triggered memories of being alone as a child. I started to think once more about the past, which I thought I had left behind.

PART ONE
THE WAR

Holocaust survivors can never detach themselves from the view that they were innocent victims of the Nazis' genocidal plan which destroyed their families and communities, leaving them bereft and in despair. In a remarkable act of courage most survivors faced the uncertainty of their future by renewing their broken lives. They married, raised children, entered trades or professions, living lives as close to normalcy as they were able. This was their answer to those who wished to annihilate them.

Another means for resisting the genocidal program was to break the silence about their ordeal, to let the world know of their suffering, to demand that their story be heard despite the deniers' attempts to erase it from historical memory.

From Victim to Witness: A Collection of the Abstracts of Holocaust Survivor Memoirs, Mervin Butofsky and Kurt Jonassohn, 2005

A JEWISH TOWN IN POLAND

My name is Oziac Fromm. I was born on June 1, 1930. I also had a Jewish name: Shaih Moishe Fromm. I seldom heard anyone calling me by my Jewish name aside from when I was called to the Torah in the Great Synagogue on the holidays. I was proud to recite the prayer wearing my father's *tallis*, prayer shawl.

I remember, as a boy, racing from my hillside home to the nearby ruins of an ancient, magical castle. The timeless fortress loomed over the town — an enduring reminder of the town's centuries of history. My family lived near the castle, on Zamkova Street. During the winter, my friends and I used to slide down the hill. It was fun going down, but when we had to climb back up, the mile-long slope was a challenge. In summers, my friends and I often played a game we called *kutchka*. It was similar to baseball, but instead of a baseball bat, we used a long wooden stick and a block of wood for a ball. My friends were both Jews and Christians. We all got along, and I was happy when I was spending time with my friends.

Both my parents' families were quite large; they numbered approximately sixty-two people. My mother's maiden name was Kissel. It was a well-known name in Buczacz because they were a prominent and charitable family. They belonged to many philanthropic organizations that helped the Jews and non-Jews of Buczacz: the unfortunate, the sick and the old.

My memories of my mother are etched in my consciousness, even after so many years. She was loving and sweet, gentle and kind, pretty and quite petite. My mother was always well dressed, and I remember her on many occasions wearing a fur coat in winter. My father would wear a fur-lined coat with a fur collar. They were an elegant and good-looking couple.

My mother was not only beautiful physically, but she was a beautiful person spiritually. She adored her husband and children — I had a little sister, Zonia — and always showered us with affection. I can remember her hugging and kissing me, although I was quite embarrassed by this in front of my friends. She was infinitely more affectionate than my father. She was also very interested in everything I did. She would sit patiently with me and help with my homework. In contrast, my father would only ask for my marks.

Aside from my mother and my grandmother, the entire Kissel family was tall. My mother came from a large family of ten children, but I had two favourites — my uncle Zigmund and my aunt Erna. Erna had no children of her own, and as a result, I was almost like a son to her, and in the troubled years to come, she would prove that devotion, becoming like a mother to me. Actually, she contributed greatly to my survival during the war.

On Friday nights before Shabbat, my mother would dress beautifully — as a matter of fact, we all did. My mother was raised in an Orthodox Jewish home, and often would get angry at my father's less observant ways. I can remember her telling us that Shabbat, a very important day, was approaching. On Fridays, all the Jews finished work early, and most Jewish stores were closed after lunch. My grandmother would come to our home before sunset, bringing traditional, homemade loaves of challah bread and a potato bread we called *bubanik*. My mother would stand at the window as the first shadows of night crept across the hill, waiting to see the lighting of the first candles by the rabbi's wife. When the first candle flared, she would turn and light her own candles. Covering her hair with a shawl, she would chant the ancient Shabbat prayers that have been repeated by Jewish women on Friday nights for centuries.

Shabbat is what I remember vividly. I was washed, and my hair was combed to the side. I wore a dark suit with a white shirt. My black shoes were shined, and I was prepared to go to synagogue with my father. Our dining room, heated by a ceramic oven in the winter, would be prepared for Shabbat with elegant dishes and gleaming silver. The dining room table was covered with a white tablecloth and dominated by a very large sterling silver candelabrum, which I still have as the one and only memento of my childhood.

My family happily gathered for our weekly honouring of Shabbat. The adult men would bless the wine, a ritual called kiddush, loaves of golden challah lay on a silver tray, and there were tantalizing aromas coming from the kitchen. Every Friday night was special. My father would make the *HaMotzi* blessing over the bread, and then everyone would receive a piece that had been dipped in salt. Every Friday, my mother made chicken fricassee, chicken soup and potato kugel. My father was always praising my mother's cooking, as she was quite an accomplished cook. We would break off a piece of *bubanik* and dip it into the sauce of the chicken fricassee. What a feast it was! I loved it.

As I mentioned, my mother was one of ten children. I do not remember all of her siblings, just the ones I was closest to. My mother's brother Zigmund Kissel was an artist, and he encouraged my own interest in art. I always enjoyed being at his side when he was drawing cartoons for the local paper. He was my inspiration and he praised my drawing. I was told that Uncle Zigmund would have convinced my family to arrange for art lessons for me, but the outbreak of war crushed that dream.

My aunt Erna and her second husband, Jacob, were also very important to me. Erna was an accountant by profession, and she worked for a large sugar company until she got married. Not long after the wedding, her first husband left for America to begin a new life for them. It was quite common in the 1930s for men of a certain age who were financially comfortable to avoid going into the army by going to America. Erna's husband literally disappeared, and no one ever heard from him again. We never knew if he had died or simply met someone else and started a new relationship. Regardless, my auntie Erna was now alone, without a husband.

When, years later, she met Jacob, a local boy, they were unable to marry because, according to Jewish law, a married woman cannot remarry unless she receives a Jewish divorce. My auntie's first husband was the son of a rabbi, and Erna and Jacob found that no one would marry them. So they endured approximately twenty years of hoping that their situation would somehow resolve itself. This was extremely difficult in a small town where everyone knew each other, and the rabbi, the leader of the Jewish community, was unwilling to marry a woman without a divorce or her husband's death certificate. My maternal grandfather, although he was an Orthodox Jew, tried to help. I remember that when he went to the synagogue to get the chuppah, the canopy under which Jewish weddings are conducted, the people there refused to give it to him. I heard my mother and father complaining about how the religious people in the synagogue were being difficult and unreasonable.

My maternal grandfather was quite a prominent person in our community. He was a religious man who served the poor and the troubled in Buczacz. He was also very resourceful, and one day he solved this ongoing problem of Erna and Jacob's marriage. He came home with four broomsticks, attached them to a bedspread, made a chuppah and married Erna to Jacob in our home.

My uncle Jacob owned a large factory in the downtown area of Buczacz where candy and chocolate were manufactured, and he also had a store in the shopping area where he would sell his chocolates and candies. He was considered quite wealthy by most, and he and Erna rented an apartment in a new building that had its own bathroom and a shower, which was something luxurious. I obviously loved to visit uncle Jacob in his factory. It always smelled so delicious, and I was allowed to eat as much chocolate and candy as I desired, as there were extra pieces and drippings everywhere. He always used to give candy to me to take home as well, and occasionally he would ask me to help him manufacture the candies. My auntie and uncle were inseparable, but unfortunately, they never could have children. I can remember that my auntie Erna gave me ten groszy weekly, which was a huge amount of money in 1938. Even my father did not give me that much.

My father was from the nearby town of Czortków, and he had met my mother through a Jewish matchmaker, which was common at the time. Matchmakers used to arrange meetings between the families of the couple, and a very important part of the matchmaking process was the dowry. The matchmaker would always address the subject of money with the girl's parents. The larger the dowry, the more important the family, and they could actually buy a more prominent husband. If a girl was wealthy, she could marry a learned man, a businessman, a doctor or a professional. But if the girl's family was poor, the potential husband would have to be a common man, from the same economic level as the woman.

As a wedding dowry, my maternal grandfather gave my father a men's clothing shop. My father would open his store every morning and close it to walk home for the main meal of the day, which was served at noon. After a nap, he would reopen his shop until six or seven in the evening. He loved to spend evenings at the coffee house playing cards and discussing politics with friends. Occasionally, my mother would have to send me there to remind him of the time.

My father believed in tough love. He rarely spoke to me, other than to ask how I was doing in school, and he never played with me. However, I know that he loved me. At that time, fathers were often aloof and demanding of their sons — believing that this was the proper way to toughen them up for what lay ahead. Perhaps he was correct. Perhaps that is why I was able to find the strength to survive the years during which I lived in constant danger.

My father was always impeccably dressed, and he would carefully select the suit that he wore to his shop each day. Tall, dark and slim, he was very good-looking. He had a collection of fedoras and walking sticks, which was the mark of a smartly dressed European gentleman in the 1930s. He took his time getting dressed in the morning, selecting the right headwear and walking stick. He was a very fashionable businessman.

My little sister, Zonia, was five years younger than me. I remember being allowed to rock her cradle when she was an infant, but I really do not remember her very well. I do not even know her Jewish name, and I cannot describe her. She was a quiet little girl, and I do not remember her crying, even under the worst circumstances. She was only four years old when the war started. Thankfully, she had very little idea about what was going on during the war.

My maternal grandmother died before the war. My grandfather owned both a factory that made men's clothing and a men's clothing store. He was a member of the merchants' committee as well as a member of the largest synagogue in the city. This synagogue was a huge, impressive structure, and my father would take me there on Friday nights and holidays. One of my father's brothers, whose name I don't recall, lived near Tarnów, where he had a medical practice, and my father would frequently travel to visit him. It was a considerable distance from Buczacz, about four hundred kilometres away. I remember that he brought back high-quality, well-made suits that his brother didn't wear any longer and, smiling, he would say, "This is not what I sell in my store." A tailor in our city used to alter the suits for my father, and I used to inherit my father's old suits. The tailor would alter them for me as well, for the holiday of Passover. I also remember getting a new pair of shoes every Passover.

Our family was traditional rather than religious, but my father was quite well-learned in Torah, and on many occasions he led the prayers in the Great Synagogue, and I stood proudly beside him. The Great Synagogue of Buczacz was regarded as one of the greatest treasures in eastern and western Galicia. The building was constructed in 1728, and that date was inscribed, in Hebrew letters and in Roman numerals, near the women's entrance. The sanctuary glowed with huge bronze chandeliers. Local artists had decorated the Holy Ark, and above the doors were the Ten Commandments, surmounted by a Torah crown. The Torah ornaments were crafted of gold and silver. The imposing historic structure was built on the riverbank.

The synagogue, unfortunately, shared the fate of virtually all the Jewish religious facilities in Nazi-controlled Poland. Its interior was completely destroyed during the occupation, and the building was in such disrepair that it was demolished after the war.

My father would take me to Czortków often to visit his family. I know he had a large family, but I didn't know them all. I knew only some of the cousins, aunts and uncles. My father's parents passed away long before I was born. In addition to his brother near Tarnów, he had two other brothers and one sister living in Czortków. I knew very little about one of his brothers, but he appeared to be an important and educated man. The other brother lived on the outskirts of the city and owned a dairy farm. There were two long buildings housing cows, and he and his family milked them by hand. On one occasion, my father and his brother forced me to drink from a pail of freshly drawn milk. They told me it was good for me, but I didn't like it. It was lukewarm and did not even taste like milk!

I attended an all-boys school on Kolejowa Street, a short walking distance from my home. When I was six or seven years old, I had a profound experience there. It changed my life and perhaps, indirectly, helped me to find the confidence and determination to survive the chaotic world in which I was about to be plunged. One day in class, a teacher, reviewing the work of the students, singled me out for praise. She had asked us to draw a book, and virtually all the others drew a simple rectangular box. My work — a three-dimensional drawing showing the book's corners and the pages in the middle — impressed the teacher. "This is how you draw a book," she told the class, holding up my drawing. "You have talent," the teacher said. It was a proud moment in my early life, and I will never forget that comment. Those encouraging words, along with the praise I received from my uncle Zigmund, set my life on a path I still follow today, with canvases in progress, a gallery and my work in dozens of collections.

And none but you and I will know
How I escaped the thrust of fate...

"Wait for Me," Konstantin Simonov, 1941[1]

---

1   From a translation by Babette Deutsch.

A CURTAIN OF FEAR

I was nine years old when World War II began with the German invasion of western Poland in September 1939. Grim news from the front and fear of German bombs sent a stream of refugees into frantic flight. The local people watched helplessly as heavily loaded trucks and horse-drawn carts rumbled through our town along with people on foot.

The powerful Nazi war machine rapidly crushed the Polish army. The Jewish population in western Poland was seized and enslaved, and most were ultimately murdered by Nazi brutes and their collaborators. However, in the early stages, no one thought that the Nazis and their thugs would be determined to destroy the entire Jewish population of Eastern Europe. The Nazi Heinrich Himmler, a leading figure in planning the Holocaust, listed the Jewish population of Poland at 3,547,896. He planned to kill every single man, woman and child.

Nazi Germany and the Soviet Union had signed a secret pact, known as the Molotov-Ribbentrop, whereby, when war broke out, the Soviets would seize the eastern half of Poland. By this treacherous arrangement, my family and the other Jews of Buczacz found themselves ruled by the Soviets. They poured over the border sixteen days after the German attack from the west, and they instituted Soviet-style rule in their portion of Poland. When the Soviet army arrived, flooding the streets of Buczacz, they began dancing in the streets, singing and playing music on their harmonicas and accordions and having a wonderful time. They were dancing with the local girls and were very friendly.

Within days, the stores were sold out of all merchandise, especially alcohol and clothing. The supply shortage ultimately put my father out of business. Stores were able to sell the goods they had on the racks and shelves, but they could not order new stock in wartime, so the stores remained empty. My father related well to the Soviets, and when the Soviet government opened a cooperative for clothing and footwear, he became its director and the manager of this division. Cooperatives were not exactly stores — they were warehouse sized and stacked with all types of merchandise, from bread and sugar to shoes and clothing. People were only able to get merchandise by using an itemized card system. For example, once a year you would be entitled to a pair of shoes and two shirts; daily, you could receive half a loaf of bread; and weekly, perhaps a piece of meat. Naturally, the line-ups at the cooperatives were extremely long. People had to wake up at 3:00 a.m. in order to line up and receive their ration of food for the day.

These were very difficult times for my family, but I experienced no antisemitism in the schools because the Soviets wouldn't allow it. To the Soviets, everyone was equal, and many younger people became impressed with the ideals of communism. While we were under Soviet occupation, we felt safe. I was never called a "dirty Jew" as I had been before.[2]

Contrary to what my father and mother expected, the Soviets were very congenial, particularly to the schoolchildren. The Soviet occu-

---

2   Under Soviet occupation, not all Jews experienced safety. Thousands were arrested and deported to Siberia, as were Polish and Ukrainian citizens. See the chapter "Soviet Power" in Omer Bartov's *Anatomy of a Genocide: The Life and Death of a Town Called Buczacz* (New York: Simon & Schuster, 2018), pp.129–157.

pation was detrimental to the economy, but for the Jewish children, it was a wonderful time, better than under Polish rule. Schools were re-opened, and the teachers were friendly and helpful. I became the teacher's pet because of my drawings, and because I was a good student. I learned to speak Russian very quickly.

All children in the Soviet Union were required to attend school. We enjoyed our classes and played a lot of sports. There was a building with a beautiful lawn with trees and flowers not too far from my school. I did not know who lived there before the Soviets came, but I now learned that it was the residence of the bishop. The Soviets removed the bishop and converted the building into an orphanage, and the orphaned children were taken off the streets in Buczacz and the small towns around us. The Soviet government dressed them neatly and cleanly, and the orphans proved to be model children and dedicated students. I was friendly with some of those orphans as we studied together for the two years that the Soviets occupied Buczacz. I don't know what happened to them after the Germans occupied Buczacz. At the time, I believed that the Russians took the children with them when their army retreated, and I was happy for them.[3]

~

Early in the morning of June 22, 1941, the Nazis attacked their former ally — the Soviet Union. The attack, named Operation Barbarossa,

---

3 "There were many Jews who tried to retreat with the Red Army into the interior of Russia. But only a few succeeded. The Russians, whose retreat was very hasty, were not interested in taking along members of the general population with them. They took only those who had fulfilled official duties during the Soviet occupation of the town. Most of the retreating Jews of Buczacz were caught by the Germans on the road." *Book of Buczacz: in Memory of a Martyred Community*, Isaac (Yitskhak) Shikhor, 1956. Translated by Dr. Rose S. Ages. See full eyewitness accounts at https://www.jewishgen.org/yizkor/buchach/buc237.html.

was the single largest invasion in the history of warfare. On the radio, Nazi propaganda minister Joseph Goebbels announced a German crusade against "the godless Bolsheviks," and panzer divisions and infantry units poured into the Soviet-held part of Poland — ultimately seizing Buczacz.

While the Germans were advancing toward Buczacz, the director of the cooperative where my father worked offered my father and our family transportation to the Soviet Union. There was little space on the departing truck, so we would only be allowed to bring two suitcases. We had to decide immediately whether we should leave or stay — the transport was leaving the following morning. My mother felt that we should stay; many people in the community did not believe that anything horrible would happen. My mother said that the Soviets had been in Buczacz for the past two years and nothing too detrimental had occurred. Our family had lost its business, but she was confident that we could eventually open another one.

We had not yet heard any stories of murder. Any knowledge of concentration camps, ghettos and the slaughter of Jews reached us only when the Germans seized Buczacz. My mother's refusal to leave was based on our families in the area, and our possessions and responsibilities. Similar regrettable decisions were to affect the lives of approximately sixty-two members of my family, including those from Czortków.

Countless families in areas threatened by the Nazis had this same reaction. People hesitated, believing that there was actually very little danger, and they, too, were quite reluctant to leave all their possessions behind. Most people could not fathom that they would be robbed of everything they possessed, or harmed, or even more unbelievably, killed. Unfortunately, that is exactly what happened. Of course, when they finally realized the truth — that everything they owned would be stolen and that death awaited the vast majority of Jews — it was too late.

My mother's refusal to leave her home and family were to cost her dearly. Her hesitancy to abandon her life was natural, but because we did not take the opportunity to flee with the retreating Russians, almost her entire family, as well as my father's, was murdered.

The Russian tanks and trucks withdrew before the Germans reached Buczacz on July 5, 1941. Before the Germans' arrival, a Ukrainian militia known as the Sich began attacking Jews and looting their homes and businesses. Their targets were Jews who had allegedly collaborated with Soviet authorities.

As German armoured units entered Buczacz, Ukrainians turned out to welcome them — strewing flowers along the town's streets and giving the Nazi salute. This reaction stemmed in part from the Ukrainians' hatred of the Soviet Union. They simplistically believed that the Germans would allow Ukraine to become an independent country; they believed that the German army came as their liberators.

For my family, and all the Jews of our town, a curtain of fear descended on our world. I was only an eleven-year-old boy, but even I became aware that our lives had been turned upside down. I can remember my grandfather anxiously descending the stairs to our apartment and my father arguing bitterly with my mother over her insistence that we stay. My mother was crying, and we were all frightened. From our home, cautiously peeking through the curtains, we looked down the road at masses of German soldiers with their panzer tanks and other vehicles. There was no escaping the threatening noise of forty-tonne tanks clanking over the roads to position themselves a very short distance from our home. The house quivered with the thudding movement of military vehicles.

Only the Ukrainians swarmed onto the streets. The Jews and Poles remained in their homes, increasingly aware that the departure of the Russians and the arrival of the Germans brought immense danger. Everyone spoke in a whisper. I could not understand it. Why were my father and grandfather talking quietly and anxiously about what was happening?

From what I could hear, there had been reports of Nazi brutality in the seizure of western Poland. When our neighbours finally did emerge, everyone was quietly exchanging what meagre, actual information they had. There were no killings in Buczacz yet, as far as we knew.

I remember my anxious mother putting a scarf around my head when I cautiously tried to look out the window; she was pretending that we were Poles. On only one occasion did we venture out. My mother took me with her when she paid a hurried visit to her sister Erna. Otherwise, we had lost all contact with other members of our family. In hindsight, I realized that my mother was probably asking my auntie to watch out for me. My father and grandfather did not dare go out into the streets.

We were trapped. Almost the entire Jewish community, swollen by refugees from other embattled areas, was now controlled by brutal German armed forces. The entire situation changed for us immediately. One day we were comfortably ruled by the Soviet Union, and the next, collaborationist Ukrainian thugs were rampaging through our town, followed quickly by the Wehrmacht. It became apparent almost immediately, even to a young boy like me, that we were now in danger. As the situation rapidly deteriorated, I could not fathom the sudden change in my circumstances. Everything I had previously learned in life would mean the difference between surviving or becoming a fatality.

Hard on the heels of the Nazis came Ukrainian nationalists. In July and August 1941, they slaughtered more than twenty thousand Jews in the Western Ukraine. The explosive hatred of the nationalists shocked even the Nazis! A few days after the Germans marched into our town, a Ukrainian police department was formed. Armed, they began patrolling the streets.

Antisemitism had flourished in the Ukraine for centuries. One of the earliest examples of massive anti-Jewish hatred occurred in the period between 1648 and 1649, when Cossacks — led by Bohdan Chmielnicki (Khmelnytsky), slaughtered between forty thousand and one hundred thousand Jews in a campaign to end Polish rule. In the period following the Russian Revolution of 1917, the Ukraine, under the rule of Symon Petliura, murdered between thirty-five thousand and fifty thousand Jews.

During the Nazi occupation, many Ukrainians — an estimated 220,000 — collaborated with the Germans in abusing and killing Jews. Ukrainians did more than collaborate — the Nazis recruited approximately thirteen thousand Ukrainians (eighty thousand volunteered to serve!) for their own SS Division. This was the 14th Waffen-Grenadier-Division of the SS. Formation of the pro-Nazi unit was supported by the Ukrainian Greek Catholic Church. At the same time, Ukrainian nationalists formed fighting units. Some fought the Germans. Some battled the Russians. Some wanted the Ukraine to be inhabited only by Ukrainians.

The Ukrainian army (the UPA) actually enlisted some Jews, particularly medical professionals. Apparently, some UPA units sheltered Jews. However, the Ukrainian units were sharply divided and often fighting with each other. Stepan Bandera, who led a nationalist group called, after him, the *Banderowcy*, had as his group's slogan: "Long live a greater independent Ukraine without Jews, Poles and Germans. Poles behind the River San, Germans to Berlin and Jews to the gallows."

The Ukrainian mayor of Buczacz, Ivan Bobyk, was a remarkable individual who did everything he could to save the Jews. The son of a poor shoemaker, he maintained good relations with the Jewish community, and even when the Germans captured our town, he opposed the establishment of a ghetto, so consequently conditions in this area were better than in surrounding districts. As a result, approximately five thousand Jews took refuge in Buczacz — bringing the total Jewish population to close to thirteen thousand. Many of the newcomers were old or ailing, but the people of Buczacz did what they could to shelter them.

But the murderous tyranny of the Germans and the Ukrainians

continued. The late summer of 1941 marked the first phase of the destruction of Buczacz Jews when the Nazis — with the enthusiastic cooperation of many Ukrainians — rounded up approximately 350 intellectuals and young men, including my father, Lieb Fromm. The Germans moved quickly, probably identifying community leaders from information seized from the files of the Jewish community.

I can vividly remember a knock on our door and my father being ordered to join hundreds of other Jewish men at the town square. He was responding to a summons to "register." One eyewitness wrote: "Over 350 men, the best and brightest of the youth and the working intelligentsia, gathered in the square. But suddenly the square was surrounded on all sides by units of the SS and the German militia, and a curfew was announced in the town. No one could leave or enter."[4]

The Nazis weren't interested in protecting professionals; doctors and lawyers were herded into a corner, while skilled tradesmen — stoneworkers, carpenters and metal workers — were all freed to be used as slave labour. We later learned that the remaining men, including my father, were forced to nearby Fedor Hill. After several hours, shots were heard coming from that direction. The men were buried in layers — some of them still alive and moaning — in a mass grave that had been dug prior to their arrival.

At the same time, the Germans told the leaders of the Jewish Council to appeal to relatives of the men and tell them that a ransom must be paid for their release. My mother and others were told that the men were all well and safe and that they were working. We were assured that letters would be possible soon. My mother relinquished all the money she had and also asked for further financial help from relatives. The ransom was subsequently paid. Unfortunately, many

---

4 From "How it Happened: First Witness." Isaac Shikhor, translated by Dr. Rose S. Ages. *Jewish Gen, the Yizkor Book of Buchach*, p. 237. https://www.jewishgen.org /yizkor/buchach/buc237.html. Other sources state that between four hundred and eight hundred men were murdered.

families were impoverished by this cruel farce, and my father and the others were already dead. All the men had been brutally murdered. A member of the Jewish community had discovered the fresh mass grave while walking on the Fedor and, horrified, informed the Jewish families about the slaughter of their fathers and sons and the Nazis' treachery. The Fedor had become and would continue to be known as the Hill of Death, a timeless symbol of terrible cruelty in Buczacz. We were devastated by the loss of my father.

This mass murder took place on August 27, 1941. Until this book was researched, I did not know the actual date of my father's death, and in Montreal's Temple Emanu-El, I had registered the date as Yom Kippur.

The Ghetto: Kaleidoscope of shifting misery and shifting chance.
Refuge of sorrows...

"El Ghetto," Alfredo Ortiz-Vargas, 1939

THE BRIDGE TO SAFETY

Throughout the autumn of 1941, members of our community were conscripted into forced labour, robbed and deprived of food and medical care. The Germans had also ordered the creation of a Jewish Council (Judenrat) and a Jewish police force. The Nazis instituted a new law in August forcing us to wear armbands identifying us as Jews.

The remaining Jews of Buczacz were forced to move to a designated area of town. Living conditions in the Jewish quarter were difficult. Our family had been allowed to carry only clothing into our new cramped quarters. Six to eight families were herded into a four-room apartment — two families to a room. Small children cried endlessly of hunger, and no one was allowed out after dark. Jews were forbidden to go to parks, marketplaces or even walk on the main streets.

My mother had to obtain food for herself, her children and her aged father. Timidly, she once approached a Ukrainian neighbour whom she knew for years, hoping to trade furniture and other belongings for food. The neighbour's cruel response was that she had no right to sell anything, that everything she owned belonged to the government. That neighbour later came and removed whatever she wanted.

Whatever items Jews had been able to save from Ukrainian and German thieves were now traded for the bare necessities of life. Furthermore, the Germans and their allies constantly tormented and humiliated people in the Jewish quarter — raiding apartments, seizing people on the streets, beating them and even killing some.

No longer could we go to the Great Synagogue, the pride of the Jewish community, where we had gathered on Friday nights. In peaceful times, our families, dressed beautifully, would walk together to the synagogue. I would be proudly holding my father's hand, and the streets were filled with so many people. This was a happy, safe time in my life. I was not only with my family, but my friends from Hebrew school were there with their families. Now the synagogue had a different meaning: to enter it meant immediate execution.

The Jewish Council assigned some work to young people, but an assignment was usually only attainable if one had connections. My first assignment with the committee was to make armbands, and although I was unpaid, I did it for the Jews who didn't know how to make their own Star of David armbands. I then made some money by sewing armbands privately. Everyone was required to wear an armband identifying them as Jews. If you were unable to make your own, one would have to be bought. I would draw a Star of David on cloth and sew it onto the five-inch by ten-inch armbands I had sewn — adding buckles that remained from my grandfather's factory. I sold the armbands to the Jewish police for food and favours. I was very resourceful. The officials gave me some work, and I was the sole supporter of my family.

Food remained difficult to obtain. My auntie Erna and Uncle Jacob helped my family and me by providing us with some food. Luckily, my aunt and uncle did not live inside the Jewish quarter. They lived at my uncle's chocolate factory. My uncle was allowed to keep his factory so that he could manufacture and supply chocolates and candy to the Germans and high-ranking Ukrainian police. The Germans would deliver sugar, cocoa and wood regularly to the factory, and since there was no other chocolate factory in or around our town, my aunt and uncle's chocolate factory kept them alive and safe for the time being.

I was then assigned to shovel wheat and rotate it constantly so that it wouldn't get too hot and rot. I can remember wearing long underwear and tying the cuffs at the ankle so that while I worked I could divert some wheat into my underwear to take home. Knowing that if I was caught doing this I would be beaten to death or shot immediately did not deter me. That was the penalty for stealing even a handful of wheat: death to the Jew. Once, I witnessed officers beating and torturing a fellow Jew for stealing a piece of bread. The officers had pictures taken of themselves afterward, in front of the almost-dead man who was lying in blood in the middle of the street. My mother quickly pulled me away from the horrible sight.

On one assignment, when I was roughly twelve years old, I was leaving work and returning home along with approximately sixty other Jewish workers when we were seized by Ukrainian police and thrown into jail. We stayed in the jail cell overnight, and the following morning the door was unlocked and we were told to get out and go outside to the courtyard. It was very early in winter but bitterly cold. The clothes I had on were not sufficient to keep me warm. Large army trucks covered with tarps were waiting outside for us. I was very scared, and I had no idea if my mother knew where I was because I had just disappeared. I'm sure she was very frightened, searching for me everywhere and not able to find me. We were pushed onto the truck, and when it was fully loaded, two German SS soldiers with machine guns came to the back of the truck and sat on the truck's bench. We all had to sit on the floor uncomfortably packed against each other. I did not mind being confined so closely to the others because it kept me warm. I don't think anybody knew where we were going, but we were fairly certain that we were going to be killed. Somehow it's possible to become resigned to your fate and feel indifferent about impending death. We tried not to think about what could happen. After some time, we arrived at another jail in another city.

This city was Czortków, where my father was born. Czortków was the headquarters of the security police for the entire region, including Buczacz. The SS and the Ukrainian police were the murderers of most of the Jews in the region. When the truck stopped and they opened the tarp and the tailgate, they started to yell and shout, "Raus! Schnell!" which means, "Out! Fast!" About a dozen SS German soldiers confronted us. Each one had a dog on a leash and held a machine gun. The dogs barked and growled frantically, ready to attack. The SS encouraged the dogs to jump and bite some of us. They then forced us inside, told us to undress to our underwear and pile our clothes in the corner. The police searched through our clothing looking for money and other valuables. They gave us some old clothing that had belonged to Jews who had already been killed. Then they forced us into cells without any food or water. I heard many of the other prisoners grimly predicting that we would all be killed.

I remember that our cell was on the ground floor and that we were all thirsty and hungry. I recall that I lowered my boot by its knotted laces through the bars of the cell to scoop up snow. I shared the snow with the other prisoners, and I will never forget how eagerly they licked snow from my dirty boot. On one attempt, an apple core became stuck to the boot, but I did not share it with the other prisoners.

I could not fully understand what was happening to me. I sincerely did not believe that I was in imminent danger of dying. I was not really capable of conceiving of death. Even after witnessing so many atrocities, I thought that only old people died. Yet the others in the cell seemed sure that we would all be killed.

For three days we heard terrifying noises: crying, yelling, dogs barking and howling, moaning and shouting. In our cell, some were saying that the police were probably torturing people to get information. Our cell door was not opened at all for those long, agonizing days. Foul smells and sick and weak prisoners are what I clearly remember.

After the third torturous day, in the morning, the police opened the door to our cell and commanded us to get out and line up in single file. They then allowed us to drink some water from barrels in the corridor. But the water was contaminated, and the majority of the people from this transport to the Czortków jail died, and others became sick.

The police herded us out of the prison. Outside, members of the Judenrat from the Czortków ghetto were waiting for us with food and hired sleighs, and they took us back to the Czortków ghetto. Nobody knew what was happening. Why had we been released?

We were able to stay in the Czortków ghetto for a few days, and I was relieved to be free from the very unpleasant ordeal in prison. In the ghetto, our names were noted, we were given some old clothing and a small bowl of food and we were told that, from the approximately sixty prisoners who were brought from Buczacz to the Czortków jail, only about twenty had been released. As I had a large family on my father's side who had been living in Czortków, I hopefully inquired about members of my family who were still alive and living in the ghetto. I was told that there were no Fromms registered, but that didn't necessarily mean that everyone was dead. There was a chance that they were in hiding. I knew that my father's family was very well known in Czortków, with many influential connections, and I prayed for their safety. I sincerely hoped that the man I spoke to in the ghetto was being truthful with me and was not lying simply in order not to frighten me. After a few days in the ghetto, the Ukrainian police herded us onto sleighs and brought us back to Buczacz.

My mother was anxiously waiting for me. When she saw me, she was overcome with emotion and kissed and hugged me. She had thought, realistically, that she would never see me again. I was very surprised to see that people on our street were happy and celebrating. Apparently, no one else imprisoned in Czortków had ever been freed. The Gestapo had somehow given permission for us to return to Buczacz, and this was the first time that this had ever happened. Previously, those who had been taken into custody were destined to die. This incident sparked the hope that the killings had stopped, but it was a fool's hope....

The most urgent priority for me now was to build a bunker to hide the three remaining members of my family — my mother, my sister and my grandfather, Moishe Kissel. The Germans and their Ukrainian collaborators raided the Jewish quarter periodically, rounding up Jews. Because I had become a favourite with the Judenrat, the committee would alert me if they knew that an *Aktion*, a roundup, was to take place. After the German-Ukrainian squads had collected their quota of Jews to be murdered, the others could warily emerge from their hiding places — safe until another sweep would take place.

Approximately two dozen Jews had constructed a hiding place in the attic of my building. I needed a hiding place for my family, so I decided to build my own bunker in our one-room apartment. I cut a hole in the wall under some steps leading to the attic. The opening was just large enough for my mother, sister, grandfather and me to crawl into. I camouflaged the entrance with a dresser and nailed it to the floor. I removed the back of the dresser and we crawled in. Then I replaced the shelf, put some worthless papers on it and replaced the plywood at the back of the dresser.

We were in our bunker under the steps when the people above us were caught, given away by the cry of a child. Mothers would keep pillows nearby, and in some instances, babies were suffocated to prevent the Nazis and Ukrainians from discovering them. Our apartment building was completely empty after a raid, but only for a short time. The next day, another few dozen people moved in.

During the raids, looters — mostly Ukrainians — grabbed everything they could find. Our hiding place was discovered when one of them, wanting to steal the dresser, ripped it from the floor. He then saw the opening to the bunker and alerted the Gestapo and the Ukrainian police. We were roughly dragged out of the bunker, and my elderly grandfather, almost blind by this time, stumbled on the steps and fell. A policeman took out his gun and then shot him in the head. He was using dumdum bullets, which expand at the tip, and I witnessed with horror the fact that half of my grandfather's head was blown away.

My mother, sister and I were thrown into jail, and we knew the consequences would be dire. My uncle Jacob, who had privileges, went to the Jewish police to ask for help, and then to the Ukrainian police, whom he knew well, in an effort to save us. They listened to his pleas, and they reluctantly consented to release the three remaining members of my family. However, since the Germans had a head count of all the prisoners, the three of us would have to be replaced by three other Jews who had not yet been caught. My uncle would have to go and find the replacements, and he refused to do so; his conscience and good heart couldn't bear the guilt.

In jail, my mother gave me the last few possessions she had — some documents from the bank and pictures of my family — and told me to keep these safe. As her eyes filled with tears, she said that I must try to save myself at any cost. I remember sitting in jail and seeing my little sister, only five or six years old then, clinging to my mother and my mother crying quietly, the tears rolling down her cheeks. Zonia was always clinging to our mother, but never crying.

We were incredibly scared and extremely hungry. In front of me was an old man, sitting on the floor, pulling out strands of hair from his beard one by one and placing them on the floor. I heard him praying to God to help him. I remember my mother repeated to me many times, "Try to save yourself." And then, "I don't know how. I can't help you, as I myself don't know what to do. I know we are doomed to die. Try to walk away when you're outside. If there is any opportunity you might have outside, just try to save yourself. Just be strong, my son, and take a chance, and God will be with you. If you won't take this chance, you will not survive. Try, my son. I am helpless, but I know that you're capable. You can do it. Just try. There is probably nobody left from our family except for us. If you follow me, it will be the end of our family. You are the only hope."

My mother made me feel important. She made me feel like an

adult, a person on whom you could depend, like a man and not a child. She continued talking quietly and constantly. She was sure that if I walked away, I would survive, and if I remained with her, I would die. She urged me to save myself and gave me the courage I needed to continue living. During the entire war, and throughout all the unimaginable hardships I endured, her words were my hope, my security and my strength to continue living. Her advice made me strive to save myself and gave me the inspiration that I needed.

Later, when I was alone in the woods, I used to talk to God. I screamed at him in my mind. When I was in a horrific situation and needed to express my pain, I appealed to God. I wanted him to help me when I needed help: when I was cold and hungry, when I was wet and living outside in the open during winter, when I was sick with a cold or a fever or when I was injured. Who was there for me to complain to? Most people have their mother, father, a member of their family or a friend. I had no one. I had only God. Sometimes I spoke loudly, hoping he would take notice. I would raise my voice as I would with my mother when I was angry. The difference was that my mother used to listen and help. God simply listened, but I felt that at least I had someone to cry to about my pitiful existence. I was extremely angry with God when I was wearing rags and was alone and starving in the cold. God is a witness to my suffering.

The next day, my mother and sister and I were forced to walk to an awaiting truck — like cattle being transported for slaughter. Not knowing where we were going, we were panicking. Hundreds of people and children were there, and the police were shouting and shooting. People were hysterical as they were falling over each other and were being separated from their families. We could not climb onto the trucks quickly enough, so we were violently pushed, kicked and beaten with clubs. I witnessed two policemen pick up a child by an arm and a leg as she struggled to climb onto the truck and throw her in like a bag of garbage.

I clearly remember Zonia's arms around our mother. Then my mother pushed me away from boarding the truck and insisted, "Now is your chance to run." I knew I could not run because if I did, I would be shot. But I stripped off my armband and began walking slowly toward the nearby bridge. The bridge over the Strypa, so familiar to me, split the city in half. It was not a large bridge, possibly fifty or sixty feet long. It was made out of wood and was only wide enough for people, horses and wagons to cross. I started to walk across and was approximately halfway when I saw an SS officer walking from the opposite side. Immediately, I froze and thought, What do I do now? Should I continue walking?

I felt in my heart and mind that he was going to kill me. My first thought was to turn back or jump into the river. The bridge was about fifteen feet above water. I had often played on that bridge with friends. We used to jump from the bridge and swim in the river, so I knew that the water was quite deep. This was a life-or-death situation. I had to make a quick decision, but my mind was blank, so I continued walking as if nothing was out of the ordinary. I don't know if I made a decision subconsciously, but my legs kept walking.

After we walked past each other, I don't know why, but I turned around, and so did he! Our eyes met and he barked at me in German, "Stop and come here!" I walked toward him as he had commanded. As I approached him, he pulled out a pistol, and I looked at him, frozen with fear.

I knew at this point that I would die. I could not move at all. He walked over to me, pointed the pistol at my head and shouted, "Are you a Jew?!"

"No," I replied in German.

Next, he demanded, "Where are you coming from?"

"I am going home from the Stadtverwaltung [city hall]. My father works there," I replied.

"Why do you speak German?" he asked.

"My father speaks German, and I go to school," I told him.

Maybe this satisfied him, or maybe he was confused. Trying to make sure he was getting the truth from me, he pushed the gun to my temple and repeated again in German, "Tell me the truth ... ARE YOU A JEW?"

"No," I replied quickly.

He put his gun back in the holster and, without another word, continued to stride across the bridge — obviously heading for the trucks loaded with Jews, including my mother and sister.

I think my mother was watching me and praying for my safety, and I believe that God was watching me too. Regardless, I crossed the bridge to safety. My mother's wish had come true. I believe that I saved myself and lived because of her last words to me. I was extremely lucky to be able to walk away from imminent death. I may have been the only living person left from this particular raid in the ghetto. There had been hundreds of people captured and brought to jail that day, all to be massacred.

I do not know who that man I encountered on the bridge was, but he obviously knew how to check if a boy was a Jew or not, and it was a miracle that he did not ask me to lower my pants. Had he seen that I was circumcised, I would have been executed immediately.

When I got to the other side, my auntie Erna was standing with others, watching the loading of Jews onto the trucks. My only thought was, Did my mother see me cross the bridge safely? I hoped that she did. It would give her strength to endure her bleak future. She would feel responsible for my survival and would be so happy that she did not witness the murder of her son. She would have certainly thought that my death was her fault.

After that incident, I did not hear any news about my mother or sister. I presume that they were murdered because my mother would have definitely looked for me after the war. I often wondered how she and my sister died. I asked myself many questions, but I had no answers. Were they buried in a mass grave or were they murdered in the

Bełżec death camp, as so many others from Buczacz were? If it was a mass grave, then where is it? Of the estimated sixty-two members of my family I lost, I have no graves to visit.

The day after the bridge incident, my aunt and I went to the cemetery to look for the bodies of family members. Bodies were lined up in rows. Other people were there too, searching for their families. It was a horrifying sight and I remember loud and hysterical sobbing and screaming. Even though there were so many rows of bodies, I could not fully believe that something like this could actually be happening. It was a sight I would never forget: so many dead bodies and in such unspeakable conditions. The heads of many had been torn open by explosive bullets, chests were ripped open and limbs were missing. The dead were of all ages, including many babies and children. The people who were killed were all innocent. They were not people who had committed crimes. They were killed because of their religion, and they were killed without remorse or pity. None of the dead were properly buried; there were no markers or graves.

I found the body of my grandfather. My auntie was crying. I was not sobbing, but tears were running down my face. This cemetery was where the members of my family had been buried, generation after generation. Some monuments were more than a century old. Later on, many of them were removed, and I heard they were used to pave the farmers' market in Buczacz. Our cemetery was now a mostly empty field, with few gravestones. The iron gate to the cemetery was also gone — stolen or sold for scrap. The cemetery for Jews did not exist any longer. Jews were now dumped into mass graves.

My aunt said a prayer over her father's body and we said goodbye to him. The caretaker of the cemetery, who was not Jewish, said that the dead from this last raid would be buried in a mass grave and the mound would be ploughed over. As a result, we do not know exactly where my grandfather is buried.

After we left the cemetery, my aunt said she had made arrangements for me to go into hiding. My auntie and uncle had also made their own arrangements with my uncle's friend, who was in the restaurant business, to share a hiding place with two other couples. She said she was sorry she couldn't take me with them, but there was a total of six people already, and she could not bring me because the others rejected the idea of children sharing their hiding space.

My uncle's friend, the restaurant owner who would end up sheltering them, was not Jewish but was his closest friend and his partner before the Germans occupied Buczacz. They were also co-owners of the restaurant's building, where the three couples built a hiding place. My uncle's friend was trusting my uncle with his life, and the three couples were trusting my uncle's friend with their lives.

Meanwhile, my aunt had arranged for me to be hidden on a farm run by a man named Jasko Rudnicki. My auntie, in her anxiety to protect me, hardly knew what she was doing, but she was trying everything possible to keep me alive. For a long time, I thought she had abandoned me; at the time, I was hurt and angry because it felt to me like she did not want me to live with her in hiding. Today I can understand her decision. I'm sure it was hard for my auntie to go into hiding without me, but she had to accept it.

PART TWO
GOING INTO HIDING

Peace is a daily, a weekly, a monthly process, gradually changing opinions, slowly eroding old barriers, quietly building new structures. And however undramatic the pursuit of peace, that pursuit must go on.

John F. Kennedy, 1963

LIVING IN THE FOREST

In the evening, before the imposed curfew, a farmer came to my aunt's home to pick me up. His wagon was filled with straw and was pulled by two horses. There were five people in the wagon already — a father and mother, their sixteen-year-old daughter and their two teenaged sons.

The family who was picking me up were friends of my uncle's from the nearby district of Potok Złoty. They were Jewish farmers and knew everybody in the area. They were also going into hiding — not too far away, I later learned — and planned to deliver me to Jasko Rudnicki. At dawn, we finally arrived at Jasko's place. Jasko had built his little home in the woods, secluded from any neighbour. A dirt road ran through a small settlement of only five homes, all with roofs of straw, and there was a small flourmill next to the small river.

Jasko's home was the first when you entered the settlement and it appeared to be a good place to hide. We were a considerable distance from any traffic, and the dirt road was wide enough for only one wagon at a time. If two wagons approached each other, one had to drive off the road and wait. As time passed, I realized how quiet the area was; there were very seldom visitors, usually only a local farmer going to the flourmill. The mill was powered by water, as there was no electricity in the area. Families had rerouted water from the river,

Sketch of Jasko's farm, by Maxwell Smart, circa 2010.

which turned a wooden wheel slowly. The shaft of the wheel had one gear, which turned around a stone and ground a small amount of wheat or corn to produce coarse flour that could then be used for baking bread.

Jasko would become my only link with the outside world. He was twenty-eight; his wife, Kasia, was twenty-two, and they had two little boys. They were poor farmers, living at the edge of the woods. Actually, they were farmers without a farm. They had only a garden plot for growing vegetables such as corn, beets and potatoes for their own use. Jasko would hire himself out to other farmers, working for them during the various seasons: there was a season to cut wheat and a season to harvest potatoes — every plant had a season for cultivating and harvesting. Jasko was not paid with money, but with food.

Jasko's home, called a *lepianka* in Polish, a mud hut, had a single window and one door. The straw roof had a little attic space where I occasionally stayed. Jasko had a stable, one cow, one pig (that he had bought as a piglet, fed during the year and would kill to eat at

Sketch of Jasko's house, view from the woods, by Maxwell Smart, circa 2010.

Christmas time) and a horse. This stable was my home during the cold winter nights.

When I slept in Jasko's attic, it was warm as a result of the heat rising from the main floor. Jasko always had some food for me — mainly black bread and sour milk, which was actually yogurt, in a jug. When I would crawl into the hay in the stable to sleep, Kasia would come in the morning to milk the cow. When I joined her, she would tell me to wait, and she would later give me bread and milk.

Kasia would dress me as a Polish boy in an outfit worn in this area: white pants made by hand from jute and a shirt embroidered with colourful cotton threads. As for my new Polish name, Jasko decided to call me Staszek, which was Kasia's little brother's name.

One day, I was delighted to encounter the family who had brought me here. They stayed in the woods most of the time, and their children were older than me, but I looked forward to seeing them in the mornings. I used to share my food with the girl. She was pretty and slightly older than me, and I think I was in love with her. I remember we used to kiss and touch.

I did a lot of work for Jasko and his wife. I learned how to milk a cow, make butter, clean the stable and make a fire in the oven. I would cut wood, hay, corn and straw for the animals. I would lead the cow out to the pasture and sometimes the horse. I remember Jasko showing me how to keep the horse from running away. He told me to bind the horse's front legs together so that it restricted him from running but he still had enough mobility to graze.

I also worked on a spinning wheel to make thread from the jute plant, and then I made trousers and shirts for the children, obviously sewing by hand. (I knew how to sew by hand with a needle, having learned this skill in my grandfather's factory.) I also made caps for Jasko, his boys and myself.

I would remove ashes from the oven and save them for Kasia. She washed their laundry with ashes instead of with soap. Kasia would put the dirty clothes into half of a wooden barrel and pour a pot of hot water over it. Then she covered the laundry with a cloth, tucking it tightly around the edges, and put a two-weeks' collection of ashes on top. She would then pour more water on top to cover the ashes. The mixture was left overnight, and in the morning she took the laundry to the river. There she used a rock with a flat paddle to beat the clothes, and then rinsed her wash in the river. Finally, she laid out her laundry flat on the ground to dry. This process resulted in clothes that were white as snow!

Once a month, Jasko hitched up his horse and wagon for the trip to Buczacz to collect his fee for taking care of me. On those occasions, he would take along produce from his garden, as well as eggs and butter, and sometimes even a chicken to sell. Jasko would carry my letters to my aunt and bring back her replies.

It was a fairly comfortable time for me. I was known in the small village as Jasko's "Zydek," his "Jew." Nobody bothered me and I was safe, I thought. Unfortunately, the happy times did not last.

One Sunday, Kasia brought me a piece of cloth and asked me to make a cap for her sister's son. While I was sewing the cap, we heard shooting in the distance. An alarmed Jasko told me to hide in the woods behind the house.

I returned in the evening and heard the tragic news: The *Banderowcy*, Ukrainian nationalists, had caught the family I had travelled with while they were hiding in the forest. For the following few days I ventured into the woods, hoping that some members of the family had survived. On the third day, I found the two brothers, Dolek and Benyick, and they ran over to me and told me that the *Banderowcy* had indeed captured their parents and sister and dragged them away. The brothers were extremely frightened. A nearby Polish farmer had helped their family, but they were now afraid to go back to the village and to that farmer. I knew that they would need food and would not survive without help, and that they must be extremely cautious. Jews were hiding in nearby forests but were endangering themselves daily in the search for food. Many farmers were hostile toward Jews; others were helpful, but wary. The penalty for aiding a Jew was death, not only for the farmer but for the farmer's entire family.

Weeks passed and then one day, without warning, I saw, through the window, Ukrainian policemen walking toward Jasko's farmhouse. Neighbours must have told the police that Jasko was hiding a Jew! I had foolishly thought that I was safe here. I had no time to plan an escape or even to be afraid. I picked up the baby and tried to leave the house, but I could see that many people from the village had gathered in front of Jasko's house. I decided that it was too dangerous to try to flee. Even if I was able to get outside, there were people watching, anticipating my death. There was only one door and one window, and the police were right in front of both.

The police knocked at the door and Jasko answered immediately. The officers took him outside and in front of the crowd declared: "We have been told that you are hiding Jews. If you do not show us where they are and we find them, we will kill the Jews and your entire family." Hearing this, I was frightened beyond belief. My hands were shaking, but luckily, holding the baby hid this from view. I thought, This is it, I've been caught, I'm going to die. They had definitely come for me, because they didn't go to anyone else's house. They had probably killed the mother and father of my two friends in the forest, so I thought that certainly they were going to kill me. I had escaped death once, but could I again?

As I stood there, frozen, I heard Jasko quickly and without hesitation say, "I am not hiding any Jews." The police then began an intensive search, scouring the barn, the attic and the small farmhouse. I just stood there, holding the baby. The Ukrainians stuck their bayonets into the empty straw-filled beds and the dirt floor. Throughout this long, stressful search, I was standing in full view, dressed as a Polish boy. I was pretending that I was part of Jasko's family, that I was his son and that the baby and the two-year-old were my brothers. It didn't even enter the Ukrainian policemen's minds that I was not.

When the police officers, the well-known brutal killers, had begun their search, I had put the baby down and pretended to help them by lifting a table, moving a chair and searching for "me." The Ukrainian police never dreamed that a young Jewish boy would have the courage to pretend to help them find me, the Jew!

After this incident, Jasko was worried and afraid; he could not believe what he had said to the Ukrainian murderers. He had replied automatically, without thinking of the consequences, and only fully realized after the policemen left how dangerous it was for him and his family. He had saved my life by endangering his own and that of his wife and children. During the war, it meant nothing to kill a Jew, especially if your own family was in danger. Most people, if confronted about hiding a Jew, would have turned us in without hesitation. It is my heartfelt belief that Jasko deserves a medal for saving my life. As I write my memoir now, I still have difficulty believing the huge risk that Jasko took by saying he was not hiding any Jews. I did not realize it fully at that time, as I was quite young, but today I think that he was an angel from heaven. He had saved my life again.

After the police left empty-handed, Jasko did not know what to do because he was afraid that they would return. So Jasko told me not to stay too close to his home in the daytime and to find a place to hide in the woods with the brothers. He was certain that one of his neighbours had reported him to the police. That person might even have been watching the scene unfold, and might not have spoken up about who I was for fear that others would know that they were the rat.

Sadly, because of this incident, I suffered a huge loss. While the Ukrainian police were methodically searching the farmhouse, I hid the precious family photographs and bank information in an unlit stove, as I knew that their discovery would identify me as a Jew. The next day, when I returned to the farmhouse in the evening, I attempted to remove them from the stove but could not find them. I told Kasia what I had done and was horrified to find out that the stove had been lit to make supper. The irreplaceable photographs, the one and only remaining tie to my parents and sister, were lost forever. These were the precious photos and documents that my mother had given me in jail, and they were gone. I would also need the information that was in the house and business documents, and the bank certificates, if I ever had the opportunity to return home.

These photographs were the last link I had to my family. They made me feel that I was never alone, that my mother was always beside me and with me in spirit. I used to hold them close to me, and they helped to somewhat reduce the unimaginable fear. I wished I still had the photos on the many nights and days when I was hiding, frightened, in the woods. I often fell asleep praying that someone who loved me was protecting me and watching over me. I was so very sad and felt so alone and lost at this time, knowing that Jasko could not keep me any longer. Not having my family photos was a loss that was forever burned into my consciousness.

Unfortunately, more tragic news arrived. When Jasko next went to Buczacz to collect his fee for sheltering me, as he had done the previous month, he was told by the restaurateur that my aunt, uncle and their friends had been discovered in their hiding place and killed, and that there would be no more money. The restaurant owner then gave Jasko a small amount of his own money and a blanket as an offering.

When Jasko returned from Buczacz without a letter from my auntie and told me the story about what had happened to her and my uncle, I felt that it was the worst possible news since learning about my entire family being murdered. I completely understood that I might also die, and I was so upset that I felt that I might be better off if I died. Then I would not need any shelter or food, or have to live with the constant fear of what might happen to me. I started to cry, and Jasko realized how hurtful his news was. Kasia came over to me and said, "Don't worry, I will take care of you."

Jasko still recommended that I stay with my two friends in the woods, as it was too dangerous to be at his home during the day. He told me that I could sleep in the barn at night when it was really cold,

and that Kasia would bring me some food. Food, I thought to myself. Without food, starving, I will become like a wild animal. I'll lose
all awareness of danger and be vulnerable and careless while looking
for food. Countless people in hiding were killed because they were
searching for food. It was not difficult to hide, but we had to leave our
hiding places to feed ourselves. If only I did not need food!

I remember Jasko showing me how to trap a rabbit. He would
tramp into the woods during the winter and set traps in the snow
where the animal tracks lay. I often caught rabbits in a trap, but occasionally I would find only half of the rabbit. The other half had
obviously provided dinner for someone else, but I was grateful they
had left some for me.

Winter was coming when I was forced to live in the woods with
the two brothers. We discussed building a shelter. We found an area
not far from the river, a little hollow space under a large rock where
we could be sheltered from rain. It was very low, so we could only sit,
and although we tried, we could not dig any deeper. It would have
been fine in the summer, but in the winter it would be horrible —
with little protection from the wind. It was not a place that could
keep us warm. We needed to find or build something that was well
insulated. Most desirable would have been a place under a rock that
extended from one of the mountains. We kept searching for a natural
hiding place, but there were no caves in our area. We realized that we
would have to build something, but that temporarily we would have
to stay near our existing shelter.

We used fallen leaves as a mattress and covered ourselves with our
coats for warmth. We would sleep closely together to provide maxi-
mum body heat. We changed positions during the night because the
centre was the warmest spot. Many nights, however, the cold was so
penetrating that we could not sleep, and even the boy trying to sleep
in the middle would be freezing.

One day, at dawn, we heard shouting. It was the Ukrainian
Banderowcy, prowling the woods, searching for Jews. Fortunately, we

discovered them before they discovered us. We grabbed our coats and ran in the only direction that we could: down a hill and into the icy waters of the river. We crossed as quickly as possible. It wasn't very deep, but it was freezing. There was also a very strong current in that particular place, and our pants and shoes became soaked. When we got out of the water, we continued running, with increasing difficulty because our clothing literally froze on our bodies, and it felt like I was wearing metal. We soon had to slow down. Then we stripped off our frozen trousers and ran almost naked, with only the coats on our backs, for approximately a kilometre, in the cold. We were very lucky that we fled from the *Banderowcy*, as they did descend the hill toward the river, but it was unthinkable that anyone would try to cross the freezing river. I am sure that they knew the precise location of our shelter and that it was not by chance that they came down the mountain where they did — somebody in the area must have known about us.

We continued running. Then we came to a barn, where we removed our wet clothing and draped our trousers on the warm flanks of some cattle. The three of us, naked, buried ourselves in the hay and remained close together, trying to keep warm.

When morning came, the barn door screeched open and a frightened Polish farmer stood there yelling, "Who is here?" Dolek rose and explained that we had been fleeing Ukrainian bandits. Even though the farmer was extremely frightened, he took our clothing into his house and then brought us bread and milk. But he told us that we would have to leave when our garments dried. We stayed as long as we could before carefully venturing out. The farmer, a Christian Pole, was a good man, but he, too, was terrified of the *Banderowcy*.

We wanted to return to our little shelter on the hill, but we realized that it was not safe anymore. The barren, leafless trees exposed our shelter almost completely, and the *Banderowcy* knew its location. We had to find a new shelter quickly, before the winter became unbearably cold. We were desperate as we began to look for a suitable place, aware of the difficulty we would encounter digging the semi-frozen ground, but we had to do our best. We agreed on a new location that was not far from the river, as this proximity lent itself to the possibility of escape.

We borrowed some shovels from Jasko and started to dig. The ground was not yet covered with snow and not completely frozen, and we had no problem finding branches to make a roof. Our new location was against the mountain and slanted; it actually looked like part of the mountain. We made an opening in the roof of branches to allow the smoke from our fire to escape, and we gathered dry wood and kept it next to our shelter. This was our new home, a place to hide from the Nazis and Ukrainians and from the cold and the wind, somewhere we could keep warm and avoid detection.

I was grateful to be able to occasionally stay in the stable at Jasko's, where it was warm and I could receive some food from Kasia in the morning when she was milking the cow. If Kasia did not need me to help her, I would leave Jasko's barn and go to meet my friends at our hiding place. When I went to see the brothers, Kasia gave me some extra food for them. The two brothers couldn't stay at their farmer's place because he was too afraid of the consequences, so they stayed only at our new shelter. They needed food daily, and apart from the meagre amount that Kasia could give them, they had to find food on their own.

One morning when I arrived at our shelter, my friends were not there. I waited the whole day, making a fire and eating some food, but they did not show up, so I went back to Jasko's for the night. I stayed at Jasko's for the next two days, and in the morning I returned to the hideout to see if the brothers were there. The place was still deserted. Again, I stayed for the day, but I began to worry about them. I returned to Jasko's in the evening, and for the next few days I kept going back to check if the brothers were there — but they never appeared again. I asked Jasko if he had heard about them, and he said that he hadn't. I never found out what happened to them. My thoughts are that they were captured, then sold by the *Banderowcy*. The Ukrainian killers would capture Jews and deliver them to the police for a reward of złoty, Polish currency, in an amount that equalled about ten Canadian dollars at the time — that was the price for a Jew. It was tragic, but I accepted the fact that they had probably been killed.

Great is the chaos all around, and fearful
And there is no refuge. What though we cry in darkness
    and we pray —
Who will hear?

"A Word," Hayyim Nahman Bialik, 1904

DEATH IN THE NIGHT

It remained extremely cold in the forest, but it was warm in the stable among the animals. Kasia would bring me some bread, milk from the cow and sometimes an onion. When it wasn't so unbearably cold and I had to return to the woods, I desperately looked for a place to hide. I deliberately never returned to any previous hideout that I had shared with the brothers, as I was too uncomfortable being there.

I could not remain at Jasko's; it was too dangerous for me, for him and for his whole family. I really appreciated Jasko's help, as I was just a boy, alone in a war, and I knew how much difficulty I would be having without his help. However, I could not continuously impose on Jasko by staying on his land. In the woods, I found a small cave-like opening approximately four feet deep, under a large overhanging rock. I placed branches, sticks and straw in front of it to protect the space from snow, wind and detection, but I left a small entrance. The grotto was so low I could barely sit upright, but it was possible to lie down. I took some straw from Jasko's barn and placed it on the ground, as well as some rags that his wife did not need any longer.

I found an old pot that Kasia had thrown out, which had a huge hole in it. I buried the old pot in a hole in the ground. Covering it with a large stone, I now had a place to store food safely from the animals. Previously, animals would find my scraps of food and run off with them. I also made additional openings in the pot and filled it with charcoal from the fire that I needed for warmth and for cooking in the daytime. If I had the luxury, I cooked a potato in the ashes of the fire. I would store any extra charcoal from the fire and add it to the pot to keep me warm at night. I remember being quite proud of myself because I had an ample supply of charcoal to keep me warm. These days, when I make a barbecue in my beautiful garden and happy surroundings, it reminds me of how precious the charcoal was when I was hiding in the woods, particularly when it rained.

The rain also brings back many memories for me because when it rained while I was hiding, I felt safe from the killers. Today, when I am driving my car and it is raining, I feel very happy to sit inside and not get wet, and I always appreciate being protected and warm. In the woods, although I was scared at night, I also felt that the night was my security blanket, that it was a time when I was safe from the Ukrainian *Banderowcy* and the Nazis.

The hardest times were when I started to think about my family. They were the only thing that still gave me the hope that I would survive. I thought of my mother and sister and hoped and prayed that they were better off than me. I somehow wasn't thinking of them as being dead, and I wondered if I was ever going to see them again. Would they recognize me? How long would it take for us to be together again? How would I survive alone?

It was very difficult for me, at such a young age, to think that I would be separated from my family forever. I used to try to convince myself not to worry, but it was almost impossible not to believe that my future was already destined and that I would have to live like this until I was captured or killed, like Dolek and Benyick. Winter was the most painful and horrible time for me because I was always cold and hungry. My only communication with people was with Jasko and Kasia now. It was so lonely, desperately lonely, not having anyone else to talk to. If I had to stay in the woods for a day or two, I really suffered from the isolation. I began to talk to myself. I simply wanted to hear a voice. I would sing songs. I felt slightly better when I was talking out loud and hearing a voice, even if it was my own.

I had absolutely no information about what was happening in the rest of the country. I would think, When will the war end, if ever? I only went to Jasko now when I needed food desperately, and I was always grateful for that luxury. I was afraid to go anywhere that was close to any other houses because I knew that it was not safe. My sadness and anguish was unbearable, and I felt that I was going crazy. As well as hunger, cold and fear, not being able to communicate with anyone else tormented me. I did not know what day it was or how much time had passed since my two friends disappeared or were killed, but it actually did not matter. I feared that my situation would never change. Almost everyone I knew was already dead, and I thought that I would probably experience the same fate. Even though my mother had urged me to save myself, she did not tell me how, and I had lost the precious pictures so I felt that she was not with me anymore. I felt like I had lost the faces and the links to my family forever. Why hadn't I gone with her? I thought. Is she better off than I am?

I spent many nights simply staring up at the sky. I imagined that I was travelling in space and time, and I would dream and detach myself from reality. I was in my imaginary world. It was almost relaxing to gaze at the sky, the treetops and the birds, in the daytime and at night. I would dream about how wonderful it must be to be a bird, flying around freely. I dreamed of my mother, my father, my aunt Erna, my uncle Jacob, my little sister, Zonia, and the rest of the family. I remembered rocking Zonia in her cradle. It was somewhat comforting to dream of my family.

It was extremely frightening having nobody around me at night, though; it was so dark in the woods. I would often sneak into Jasko's barn, deathly afraid that someone would find me, beat me, torture me and then kill me. Staying totally alone was going to be impossible if I was to survive. I knew that I had to find other people to live with who were also hiding in the woods, and that I would eventually have to leave Jasko. He was so kind and he felt so sorry for me and always shared his meagre amount of food. I needed to ask Jasko if he had heard of Jews being sheltered in nearby woods because I couldn't live in a world of silence any longer.

I spent much of that winter alone, roaming the woods. My clothing was torn, my shoes had come apart and I used rags to cover my feet. I did not look like a Polish boy anymore. I resembled a beggar, and beggars in that place and time were, more often than not, Jewish.

Many lonely weeks passed. It felt like the seasons would soon change. I would welcome the first signs of spring. Farmers would plant their crops, and I would be able to walk barefoot. The soles of my feet were hardened, tough as leather. I could soon steal potatoes, carrots, onions and corn from farmers' gardens — but I would be careful not to damage their tiny plots. I would steal only what I needed to stay alive. It was much easier to live in the woods in the summer, hidden among the trees and greenery.

However, I still had no one to speak to. Jasko told me that there were Jews in another village about fifteen kilometres away, but he advised me not to go there. He was worried that I would get lost, or caught. I think he understood how hard it was for me to be alone. I would often ask Jasko about the war, and who was winning. He would always reply that the Germans were losing, but it certainly didn't feel like it and I didn't believe him He told me to try to be patient, that the Germans really were losing the war and it wouldn't be long until I would be able to return home. It was so kind of him to say that. He actually cared about me. I would try to convince myself that I was not completely alone because I had Jasko; wasn't I lucky?

Jasko was a mensch, a good person, but reality reared its head quite quickly when I returned to my hiding place. The only sounds breaking the grim silence of the forest were the chirping of birds and occasionally the cry of an animal. It seemed that I was the only human being on earth, and I had an abundance of time to think. I became intensely aware of the world around me, and I would imagine shapes and dream of travelling through endless space. I created my own little world of safety.

In this private world of my own mind, I would not have to hide like some small animal. When I heard the birds and saw squirrels scampering, I envied the fact that even a squirrel had a home somewhere on this earth and that it could run freely. I envied all the animals because they had homes and families and I didn't. I envied the beggar slumped on the church stairs in town because he was not afraid that someone would kill him. Why is it, I asked myself, that I am condemned to live with more fears than a beggar?

My thoughts would turn to my family, particularly if I happened to know it was a Friday night, Shabbat. I would tell myself repeatedly that just because my family was not with me it did not necessarily mean that they were dead. I thought that since I was still alive and not with them, that they might be alive too. I believed, with certainty, that my aunt was no longer alive because otherwise she would have written to me. I prayed that my sister was still alive, but I knew that it was doubtful that she had managed to survive. At the same time, I was painfully aware of reality: the chances of anyone from my family being alive were extremely slim.

Throughout all my hardships, I also remembered the happy times in my life before the war. I remembered skipping *cheder*, Hebrew school, and the time when the rabbi came to my father to be paid, asking why I had not attended Hebrew studies for several days. My father punished me for not attending classes, and I have not forgotten that beating — even today — and I even wish that he was here to beat me again! At least I knew that the pain I suffered was given from love and consideration, not from hate. I recalled the time that I ran away from home. It was actually only next door to my friend Hayalah's house for a few hours, but my mother had been frantically crying and searching for me. She never told my father about it.

Was I going crazy? Or was I already crazy? The only thing I knew was that there was no one around to love me and I had nobody to love. There was no one to care for me and to miss me, to be concerned about whether I lived or died. Except for Jasko, who liked me, the local farmers would have been happy to get rid of me, the little Jew who invaded their gardens to steal food.

I even started to hate myself. Why was I a Jew? Why were my parents Jewish? Why was I brought up this way? If I wasn't Jewish, I would not have to live in constant fear. I had no real idea of Hitler's plans. Why were we being killed? Were Jews meant to be hated and killed? Why would God make Jews if their only burden was to suffer? I would look up at the sky, hoping God was listening, and I would scream to make sure he was. Was it better to be Christian? Everyone who was Christian was living in their homes and had food and clothing, so their God must be better than mine. Their God takes care of his people. Why was my God not taking care of me?

Do you see how I look, God? I would ask. I don't even look human. I do not wash my face. I do not wash my body. I smell. I do not clean my clothes. I do not undress to go to sleep. My hands are numb and cracked from the cold. I am a dirty Jew. I am an animal. I drink water from the river, scooping it up with my dirty hands like an animal. I am barefoot. My feet are bleeding because now I don't even have rags to wrap around my feet.

Once, when I slept, I was awakened suddenly. Like an animal, I was always on the alert for intruders. But this was no prowling killer. It was a very small boy wandering through the bushes. He appeared to be younger than me and was very frightened. As he walked, he would cautiously look to his right and left. I came out of my grotto slowly and spoke softly and told him not to be afraid. I told him that I was Jewish, as he was. I could see that he was starving and trembling with fear, so I gave him a small piece of bread and he swallowed it quickly. When I saw that he felt more comfortable with me, I asked him where he had come from. He had been walking for two nights, he told me. He had started to wander when, after two days, his father did not return to their hiding place. He was certain that his father had been killed.

The boy, who was a few years younger than me, was named Janek. I am not completely sure, but I believe that his family name was Aranow. He told me that the only food he had eaten in two days had been berries and mushrooms because he had been too afraid to approach a farm. Once more, I realized my good fortune in having the help of Jasko. I felt almost happy — the happiest I had been since my two friends had been killed. I had someone to talk to again! My nights and days alone were over, and so were Janek's! We spoke for a long time and I told him that I wanted to be an artist or own a store like my father had. He told me that he was a whiz with numbers, so we played some mathematical games. I tested him by asking him to add or subtract, and he would think carefully, calculate and say the correct answer. I would check his answers by writing with a piece of charcoal on a stone.

Janek told me that his father had been an accountant in the city where they lived, but his family had fled to nearby Kolomyja to hide with a farmer. Sadly, after a short time, the frightened farmer asked them to leave. His family stayed hidden in the woods, but one night, when his mother left to search for food, she never returned. His father would secretly venture into the village to try to find something for them to eat, but one evening he too did not come back.

I told Janek I was thinking of becoming a Christian because then maybe my life would be better. My problem was that I didn't know how to convert. I knew that if Janek and I became Christians we would not have to hide anymore, and my new friend thought that it was a brilliant idea. He added that someone might adopt us, and we could live in a house. I decided that I would soon ask Jasko to help us, and if we were lucky, he might even become my father if I were Christian.

Janek and I planned to build a new bunker. I went to Jasko's home to borrow his shovel, and we searched the woods to try to find a safe spot to build our hiding place. In my current hideout, it was impossible to dig because of the rocky ground. After days and weeks of searching, we finally found a place that we thought would be safe. The location was between two large rocks — each about six feet high — that were adjacent to a mountain. It was a narrow space and was only large enough for the two of us to lie down in. We managed to dig deep into the earth between the rocks. We made our bunker approximately four feet high, with three of those feet underground. We then took large, thick branches and placed them parallel to each other for the roof.

We camouflaged the roof with layers of tree branches, straw and leaves so that it appeared to be an extension of the hill. We worked hard to make sure that the roof did not leak. The entrance was very small, and we had to crawl on our hands and knees to enter. We used an old sack filled with leaves to keep the cold out, and we found an old, dead tree trunk to disguise the entrance.

Inside, we laid straw on the ground. We had learned that we should never start a fire near our bunker. We would warm ourselves at a fire only if it was quite a distance away, and we changed the location of the fire daily to avoid detection. We always brought the charcoal left over from the fire into our bunker and made sure to have a supply of charcoal in the bunker to keep us warm. Kasia's old pot was attached to the roof of our dugout, and we would blow into it through the holes of the pot to ensure that the charcoal would burn. We would add more charcoal if it was very cold, and when there was a severe storm, we did not leave the bunker at all, except to search for food. When we did leave, we always covered up our footprints in the snow, to avoid detection. Each night, we would strip off our clothing and leave it on the snow so that in the morning we could shake off the lice.

Janek was a small boy — much smaller than I was. I was only two years older, but I often felt like I was his father because I had already been through so much. I felt responsible for him. He was always frightened. I would leave the bunker only to bring water from the river, to cook or to make a fire. He remembered, painfully, how his

Sketch of bunker, by Maxwell Smart, circa 2010

parents had left their hiding place and never returned. I was so over-joyed not to have to be alone anymore, and I genuinely considered Janek to be my family now. Janek was convinced that he was going to die, and he often depressed me — but I never completely believed that I would actually die. My mother had told me to save myself. She told me to live, and I obeyed her.

I was hungry and tired, but I sensed that I could and would ac-complish something, although I had no idea what that would be. I never knew the time — other than the rising and setting of the sun — the date or even the year because those things weren't important to me. The only necessities in my life during the war were to have food, to be warm, to hide, to not be killed and to survive the day. I thought and behaved like an animal — running instinctively when I heard a noise. I wanted to live, and I think I acted on instinct — the instinct of survival — similar to the behaviour of an animal in that when it hears a noise, it immediately feels endangered and runs, even if it does not know why.

~

One dawn, we woke to screaming, crying, shooting and pandemonium. We were too terrified to leave our bunker because it had snowed the previous night and we did not want to make any tracks. Our bunker was very well hidden, and we had stored some food and had some charcoal to keep us warm for a few days.

After it had been quiet for a few hours, we decided to go outside and investigate. We carefully peered past the branches masking the entrance to our shelter. It was quiet, and fresh snow had fallen, so the area around the bunker was all white with snow. I turned to Janek and asked what he thought all the shooting was about. We left the bunker and began to walk. I took one of the branches with me to fill in the tracks made by our feet in the snow.

We walked cautiously toward the river, but when we reached the riverbank we saw a horrifying sight. There had been a complete massacre! The sight was so horrible that we could barely look at it. The snow was completely stained red with blood. There were bodies scattered everywhere. The people had probably been running away from the *Banderowcy*. Janek insisted that we get out of there quickly because they might still be close by.

What kind of people could be so cruel? I thought. In my experience, the Ukrainian nationalists hated Jews even more than the Germans did. The Germans allowed them the freedom to kill Jews without any rules or restrictions. The nationalists were not fighting a war of independence for their country. The Jews had not occupied their country or overthrown their government, so why did they kill? Just for the pleasure? If all the Jews were dead, who would be next? How could people be so indifferent, so barbaric and filled with so much hatred toward Jews? This killing site was horrific and beyond belief.

I realized that eight people had built a bunker not too far away from ours, and we absolutely did not know anything about it. We checked the area and found that their bunker was quite large, and I was shocked and impressed at the sight. One could practically stand upright in it. It was very well-built and really organized. The wood that they built the bunker with had been cut with a saw. When we needed wood, we would collect broken pieces at random, whatever we could find lying in the woods. Since we did not have a saw, we haphazardly placed them next to each other. In contrast, their wood pieces were well-made and the bunker was well-camouflaged. We would never have discovered the location of their bunker, although we must have passed it several times. How did the Ukrainian *Banderowcy* find the bunker? They must have been informed. It would have been extremely difficult to have randomly found a well-hidden bunker in the woods. I believe that it may have been a farmer who supplied them with food or the tools that had helped them build their bunker. They would have needed a large quantity of food to feed eight people, but whatever the reason, they were ultimately found.

We were just two young boys who needed guidance as we thought about what to do with so many dead bodies. Do we leave them here? We wondered. Do we bury them in the bunker? We both decided that we needed their clothing and shoes, as we had no shoes at all and our clothing was torn and full of holes. We were literally wearing rags, and their clothing was in relatively good condition.

Were we scared being surrounded by dead bodies? I wasn't — I knew that they could not harm us. I had seen dead bodies before, but it was a new experience for Janek. He had a shocked, blank stare on his face, as if he was in a trance. He was so frightened by this massacre that I had to shake him violently back into reality. I kept yelling at him to come and help me move the half-frozen corpses. I had decided to drag their bodies into their bunker and remove some of their clothing, specifically, shoes, pants and coats. We were lucky that their bodies were not completely frozen yet, or we would not have been able to remove their clothing as easily. We found useful utensils in their bunker: metal spoons, forks and knives. We had only one wooden spoon, which I had made myself, so we eagerly took what we needed.

It was a terrible experience to move the dead bodies, inch by inch, into their bunker. There was no front door; there was only a camouflaged entrance not larger than a small hole to crawl into. So Janek went into the bunker, and I pushed the bodies toward the entrance. Then he pulled the bodies into the bunker from inside. Before that, though, we had to gather all the bodies and bring them to the entrance. It was a long, difficult, tiring process. Some of the bodies were lying face up, with their eyes still open. Many were covered with snow and splattered with blood, and blood covered our hands. It was exhausting pulling all the bodies because they were so heavy. It was also very difficult to remove the few pieces of needed clothing, but somehow we managed. All the while, we were shivering from the cold. When all the bodies had been moved into the bunker, we blocked the entrance with branches to prevent any animals from entering, and then we were ready to leave. This horror is etched indelibly in my memory and I cannot erase it.

I don't know why I turned around before we left the area, but I did, and I noticed a body half-submerged in the river. The river was approximately forty feet wide, and its banks were encrusted with ice and were very slippery. The river wasn't too deep, but the current was strong so the centre of the river was not frozen. It appeared as though a woman had been fleeing and had reached the other side of the river but had been shot in the back. Half of her body was sticking out of the river and the other half was covered with snow. Janek and I did not know what to do, and we debated the benefits of leaving as quickly as possible. But as I was looking at the body, something moved! The woman was alive! We felt that we had to go to the other side and help her. Our morality wouldn't allow us to leave a person who was still alive in the water; we had to try to help her. I can remember Janek crying and saying that the water was too cold, that he was freezing and afraid that he was going to die. I grabbed his hand and together we plunged into the water, clinging to each other so that the current wouldn't overpower us. We were so cold that our bodies became numb, and I wasn't sure that we were going to make it. But we crawled over the ice and sloshed forward until we finally reached the other riverbank.

I could see immediately that it was not the woman who had moved. It was a very small child who was probably only two years old. Her entire body was completely covered with snow, but she was held there between her mother's frozen arms just above the water. It was incredibly lucky that she had not frozen to death — her mother's dead body had sheltered her from the wind, and she was somehow still alive. I couldn't believe that she had survived. When the baby heard us, she started to cry hysterically. It was difficult to remove the baby from her mother's frozen arms, but I succeeded. Every minute that we stayed in the freezing water increased the danger to us, so with the baby held to my chest with one arm and Janek holding the other arm, we quickly crossed and exited the cold river. We had to leave the body of the woman on the riverbank exactly where she was found.

Of course, now our clothing was completely frozen, but we were very lucky that we hadn't already changed into the clothing that we had removed earlier from the dead bodies. We crawled into the large bunker, and it was much warmer than it was outside. We then undressed the baby and ourselves as quickly as possible and threw our old and wet clothing over the corpses. We re-dressed in the dry clothing that we wanted to take to our bunker. It was such a relief to be dry and relatively warm. We sat close to each other to try to warm up, and we placed the still-crying baby between us so that she would be warm too. The dry clothing was warm, but all the shoes, though in reasonable condition, were much too big. I wrapped some rags around my feet so that the shoes wouldn't fall off my feet. I was overjoyed to finally have shoes because I had worn rags on my feet for such a long time.

We needed to make a fire so I searched the bunker for anything that I might have missed earlier as we had been distracted while bringing the bodies inside. Now I noticed that this group of people had many more possessions than we did — pillows, blankets, pots, candles and matches — so we took everything that we were able to carry. During our search we also found cooked potatoes, some flour, onions, two loaves of bread and half of a sack of potatoes. This was enough food for the two of us to feed ourselves for a few weeks. What a treasure! Unfortunately, it was at the expense of other people's deaths.

By this time, the sun was starting to rise. We found some dry wood behind the bunker and started a fire. We took one of their pots and filled it with snow, sliced the cooked potato, added flour and waited for the soup to boil. The baby was still crying, and we concluded that she must be crying because she was hungry. Before the water boiled, I gave her some cooked potato and she stopped crying! We all ate, and thankfully, the baby fell asleep soon afterward. Janek continued to shiver and couldn't get warm, no matter how many layers of clothing he wore. He wanted to return to our bunker, so we walked with the baby through the freezing woods. Once more, we had to be very careful because it was snowing, and we didn't want to leave footprints behind.

When we got to our bunker, it was warm, and the charcoal was still lit in its hanging pot. The baby ate some of the soup that we had made and fell asleep once again, but we had to decide what to do with her because we could barely care for ourselves. I decided to approach Jasko for help because there might have been a chance that he could take the baby and care for her. When I asked Jasko for advice, he replied that we should search the woods for other hidden Jews who might care for her. He explained that the baby could pose a serious problem, as her crying could make our or their detection much easier. Kasia told me that they were definitely unable to care for the baby because everyone would know that it was not hers. We agreed that the best idea would be to look for other Jews that were in hiding nearby. I asked Jasko if he knew of any other villages where Jews might be hiding. He did know about some Jews hiding out in Polish villages not too far from our place. He was fairly certain that I would find some Jews who might agree to care for the child, even though the crying child may have been the reason that the others were found.

Unfortunately, the baby girl cried very often. She was frightened, obviously, and wanted her mother. We really didn't know what to do with her. That night was so difficult because the little girl hardly stopped crying, and Janek could not stop shivering; I think he caught a cold from the freezing river. We were very scared. We thought that the baby might be sick, and I remembered my mother's words regarding other women carrying pillows into the bunkers in the ghetto. There were horrible stories of mothers having to suffocate their own children so that the crying didn't alert the Nazis or Ukrainians to their hiding place.

Then I remembered that when my little sister had cried in the crib at home, my mother always checked her diaper. We unbundled the child and she was soaked with urine and feces and smelled vile. We did not know exactly what to do and we did not have water to clean her with. I threw out the spoiled rags that had been used as diapers for her, and I cleaned her with some of the rags that I brought from their bunker and bundled her up again. She stopped crying.

I decided that I would begin a search for people who could care for the baby the next day. When I woke up, I dressed warmly, put a boiled potato in my pocket and started walking. I had ventured out for perhaps two miles when I heard the sounds of a bell on a horse-drawn sleigh. I wrongfully assumed that it was a friendly farmer and thought that maybe I could get a ride. Unfortunately, it was the Ukrainian police. They rode beside me looking closely at my face, then cheerfully yelled, "We've caught a Jew!" They tied me up to their sleigh, and since I could not run as fast as the horse, I was simply dragged. Interestingly, it was actually easier to be dragged than to run as the ground was covered with a few feet of snow.

After a while, we stopped at a house where a girlfriend of one of the policemen lived. He was proud to show her that he had captured a Jew, knowing that he would receive a reward for this task. She came out of the house and looked at me with sympathy. She then turned to him and asked what he was doing. She said that I was just a boy and begged to have me untied and brought me into the house. How lucky I was! This young woman saved my life; she saved me from being imprisoned, beaten and possibly even killed. My entire body was hurting from the dragging, and my hands were bleeding badly from the ropes that had been tied onto the sleigh. This kind woman brought a small cloth, cleaned my bleeding wrists and bandaged them. All the while, she was yelling and arguing with the policemen for doing something so cruel to a child. I kept thinking about the problems that I had now simply because I had saved a baby girl. When she had finished bandaging my wrists, she opened the back door of the house and told me to run into the woods. I quickly ran out of the house and did not look back, even though I suspected that the police would shoot me in the back, the way the mother of the young child we rescued was shot.

I stopped at a nearby *lepianka* to ask if anyone knew where any Jews were hiding. At one of the houses, a woman did not let me in, but she gave me a piece of bread and responded that she didn't know, all the while pointing in a certain direction.

Shortly after I had left that house, a man came running after me and asked where I was from. He was Jewish but was not dressed like a Jew; he was dressed like a Polish farmer. It seemed to me that he had come from the house of the woman who had given me bread. He asked me what I was doing here, and I told him the entire story of the people in the bunker and the baby. He led me deeper into the woods, and it seemed that he was familiar with the area. We approached his bunker, which looked like a natural extension of the mountain, similar to the one Janek and I shared, and we went inside, crouching to get in. I met some Jewish people sitting inside on straw, on the ground. I recounted my story and said that I needed help with the child we had found, and then described where the large bunker was located and how I had found the baby. One man mentioned that he had helped build that bunker, and he motioned for me to wait while he went outside. He quickly came back with a woman who was hysterical and crying, saying that the baby was her sister's. They had a discussion among themselves and decided to depart the next morning.

It was really comforting to me to listen to adults making decisions and telling me what to do. Experienced people knew so much more than I did. They were talking about the war and saying that it was almost over, with the Germans retreating rapidly, and I thought that maybe I would live to see the end of the war and return home. They advised me that I would have to be very careful now because the Ukrainians were very angry; they had to retreat with the Germans or be arrested. They also informed me that in the woods, around this particular village, there were approximately fifty to sixty Jews in different bunkers.

The Jews who were hiding near the village were working with the Polish farmers to protect the area from *Banderowcy*, whose goal was to burn down all the Polish villages. The Poles and the Jews would be on guard throughout the night. It was very interesting to listen to their conversations. Jews were helping the Polish Christian farmers, and in return, the farmers would help the Jews. I decided that it would be a good idea for Janek and me to stay with them because both of us needed the support of adults.

The Jews in this bunker were cleaner; all of them had shoes and nobody was wearing rags. I had not seen so many Jews in one place for so long, and I was anxious to meet them all. There was a chance that someone would recognize me and hopefully even know a member of my family.

In one of the bunkers, we ate a piece of bread and a hearty soup made with corn flour, and then went out to stand guard for the village. When it became dark, they gave me a stick and a metal pail, and I was told that if I saw or heard anything, I was to start making noise immediately. I did not see anyone other than Jews. They guarded the village from various locations, and they worked all night. After we had been outside for about two hours in the cold, some farmers came out and invited us into their home. They gave us food, and we stayed in their house warming up. We had some homemade alcohol, went back outside for a few hours and then returned to the farmer's house again to get warm. I was so happy to be with those Jews. They were organized and there was a feeling of community. I asked when they could start caring for the little girl, and if Janek and I could please stay with them. We went back to their bunker at dawn to rest, and they informed me that I would be awakened when the group was ready to leave in the morning. Seven or eight people, all adults, lived in their bunker. They told me that many of them were related.

They woke me in the morning, and we prepared ourselves for the journey to retrieve the baby. I walked on the main road, but they would only use hidden paths in the woods. It took us most of the morning to arrive at the bunker where Janek and I had sheltered the bodies. I also showed them the dead body of the woman across the river, still there with half of her body in the freezing water. I recounted the story about Janek and me crossing the river and taking the baby and how, unfortunately, we could not take the woman out of the water because it was too hard for us. They understood, and without hesitation, two men entered the water and removed the woman. The woman's sister started to cry when they brought her body into the bunker. They wanted to collapse the bunker to avoid its detection, but it was too difficult because it was well built, so they decided to leave the bodies where they had been placed inside, and they simply blocked the entrance completely with branches and rocks and anything else they could find.

We then left and walked over to my small bunker, where we found the baby, sitting beside Janek. He complained that he still felt really cold and was not feeling well at all. I asked some of the people to see if they knew what was wrong with him. They said that it seemed like he had a fever, and I explained that he had probably gotten sick while in the water trying to save the baby. I appealed to them again, asking them to allow us to stay with them in their bunker, but they refused, saying that their bunker was too small for two more people. They promised that they would ask some people in another bunker if they had space for us. I begged them to help Janek, and they told me to give him hot water and keep him warm, and because he was young, they said, he should be fine. They left with the little girl, but I do not remember the child's aunt saying "thank you" to me for saving the baby. This baby had been so much trouble for us, but I had a feeling that they were angry with us because they did not leave us any food. They had seen that Janek was very sick and knew that it was because he had tried to save the child. Ukrainian police had almost killed me dragging me by a horse-drawn sleigh, and my body was still hurting and my hands still raw from the ropes. They seemed not to appreciate what we had done; they appeared indifferent and devoid of emotion. In hindsight, I thought about how much easier our lives would have been if we had not tried to save the baby, but I absolutely could not have let a baby die. I was certain that she would be a huge problem for them because she had created so many problems for us.

I was also sick, although not with fever. I had developed an infection in my left leg and it hadn't healed at all. I suspect that it was from an insect bite that I had scratched and made worse. I could not keep it really clean and I didn't have any medical supplies, so it was always oozing. I asked Jasko if he could recommend anything that would help it heal, and he told me to apply a particular leaf. As long as I could walk, I thought, and the pain was minimal, I believed that I would be fine. When I was liberated and a doctor treated me properly, the situation improved, but the damage had been already done. My leg had been swollen from the ankle to the groin before treatment. I've had to wear a support stocking since then.

It was a relief to be alone with Janek. We stayed in and around the bunker. We had food and clothing, and used all the clothing that we weren't wearing to cover the ground that we slept on, as it was always damp inside. We were relatively safe, and the fresh snow was protecting us because there were no tracks leading to our bunker.

It was extremely cold outside, and Janek appeared not to be getting better. He looked flushed and felt like he was burning up. I kept giving him water and trying to keep the bunker warm. After a few more days, I told Janek that I needed to leave at night when he was asleep, go to Jasko and ask him what he could do to help. He could hopefully get him some medication, and then I would return in the morning. I really did not like to go out in the dark even though I was not afraid of the animals, since they were smaller than I was, and I never saw any large animals, where I was hiding. At night, walking between trees made me anxious, to say the least. The wind blowing through the bare tree branches made strange and scary noises, but I continued to walk, trying to convince myself that I was not afraid.

The distance from our bunker to Jasko's house was only a few kilometres, but in the dark, cold winter, through thick bushes and branches protruding from the soft spots in the snow, it was a difficult walk and I would fall down quite often. Many times, I felt like staying on the ground and actually giving up.

Little Janek would rarely leave the bunker because he was so afraid, and although I did not mind walking the distance when needed, it was agony to be alone. I felt that I never wanted to be alone again. I was quite afraid most of the time; I was not a hero, I was a boy, not much older than Janek, but I tried to be like a father to him, and he relied on me like a father, a protector. Hopefully, Jasko would know what to do. It was cold that winter, very cold, and the charcoal that we used to warm the bunker was running out quickly. I knew that I would need to make a fire when I returned.

When I arrived at Jasko's, he was not there but Kasia was very busy. Jasko had recently killed their pig and Kasia was cutting and preparing it for Christmas, which was only a week away. I think that Jasko ate meat only once a year. Kasia asked me to help clean the stable, remove the manure and lay down fresh straw. She brought me some food, and I remember that it smelled so incredibly good that I temporarily stopped worrying about Janek. Jasko came home late. He was drunk, and Kasia asked me to stay so that I could help her in the morning. She was a good cook and I was enjoying myself. I ate and even had a drink with Jasko. I related the whole story about the baby and Janek's high fever. Jasko said that it might be scarlet fever and that he would go to the town to try to get something to help him. As it was already very late on the second night, I went to their barn to sleep instead of making the long trek back to my bunker. Kasia gave me a blanket because it was unbearably cold, but I kept thinking of Janek, alone in the bunker and sick. I knew that he would go crazy, not knowing where I was and if I was coming back.

In the morning I told Jasko that I had to return to my hiding place because Janek was alone in the bunker. They gave me some food, and I walked back to where I had left Janek, but when I arrived I found that the entrance was exposed, the charcoal was not lit, it was cold inside and Janek was not there. I looked around and nothing was missing. It had snowed that night, and quite a bit of snow had drifted into the bunker. I am not sure when, but Janek must have left the bunker while I was gone. I cleaned up, closed the entrance, filled the old pot with charcoal and lit it.

It was getting warmer inside, but I knew that I had to find Janek. I wondered where he could be, so I checked all the places we used to go to. I went to the river where we went for water, but he was not there. I took the path that led to Jasko's because I thought he could have been looking for me, but I could not find him. I tried another path, and there was still no sign of him, so I returned to the bunker to eat some food. It was still daytime, so I hoped that he would return shortly. I waited and waited for him, but I had a strange feeling that something had happened. I worried that because he had a high fever, he might have gone outside to cool off, but I was certain that he wouldn't have gone too far. I went outside to search for him again, but it was getting very cold, so I returned to warm up.

After a short time, I went out again to look for him. This time I went to the far side of the bunker where we never went, and a short distance away, I discovered him lying on the ground covered in snow. I saw only a small part of his body where the wind had blown the snow away. I immediately dragged Janek into our bunker where it was quite warm now. I tried to pick up his hand but could not because it was stiff, and I checked his forehead to see if he still had a fever, but he felt like a block of ice. I made the bunker even warmer, but he still didn't move at all. I prayed that he wasn't dead because I really didn't want to be alone again. I decided to leave him in the bunker and return to Jasko to ask him if he had found any medicine that could help Janek. I didn't want to bother Jasko, but I really had no choice since I did not know what to do. Luckily, Jasko was home. For the very first time, Jasko offered to go to the bunker with me. I was quite surprised and now somewhat worried because he had never come in the past. When we reached the bunker, he was astounded that I had built such a well-camouflaged bunker, and he praised me.

When he went into the bunker, he came out immediately and told me that Janek was dead. I was shocked, and I didn't know what to say because I had not expected him to say that. I started to cry, and when I looked at Jasko, I saw that he was crying too. He sympathized with me because he knew how much Janek had meant to me, and he knew how desperately I had wanted to revive him.

Once again, I was alone. I knew that I couldn't live entirely alone again, and I was determined not to. I would look for and find the people from the village, specifically the auntie of the baby that Janek and I had saved, hoping that she would let me stay with her. I pitied myself and was lost in my sorrow and loneliness. Jasko did not collapse the bunker; he just blocked the entrance more securely. This time, we sealed the bunker, leaving Janek inside on the hay; the bunker became his grave.

Even in the most barbaric times, a human spark glowed in the rudest heart, and children were spared. But the Hitlerian beast is quite different. It would devour the dearest of us, those who arouse the greatest compassion — our innocent children.

Emanuel Ringelblum, 1942

WANDERING BEGINS

Jasko tried to reassure me that the Soviets were advancing and the Germans were retreating and that it would not be long until the war would be over. I had difficulty believing him and thought that if freedom was coming soon, why did Janek have to die? I was heartbroken, and again I asked God, "Why?" I was so angry about Janek's death, and despite being close to freedom, I cried loudly, out of anger as well as sadness.

Christmas was approaching and Jasko told me that the Ukrainian police had departed and that I could stay in his house again. Months passed. Then one night, he came home drunk and excited, telling me that the Soviet army was in Buczacz and that I was free and didn't have to hide anymore. When I heard the news, tears started to roll down my face, and I kissed him and ran over to Kasia. I hugged her and then asked if it would be possible if Jasko could take me back to Buczacz.

We left for the city at the beginning of April 1944. I was almost fourteen years old, and I was so lucky to be liberated. I had defied the odds and survived and saved myself. I believed that my mother had somehow contributed to my survival.

I can remember sitting on the wagon with Jasko on the front bench, not hidden, like a normal human being, and for the first time in all the years of war, I felt no fear. There were no Germans, no Ukrainian police, no *Banderowcy*. I was not just a Jew anymore. I was a human being. It was so dramatically different than the way that I had come to Jasko, in the back of the wagon, hidden and covered with hay.

My years in hiding had been horrible, nightmarish. As we were driving, I dared to hope that someone in my family was waiting to greet me. I felt so close to freedom now. I told Jasko that if anyone in my family was still alive, they would reward him. But freedom did not happen as I had hoped. About five kilometres from Buczacz, we saw that German planes were still attacking the Soviet army and that the Soviets were retreating.

The city of Buczacz, my city, had been liberated at the end of March, and I thought I was going home. It was now re-occupied by the Germans, though, and this time, circumstances were even worse. The front line of the war ran through Buczacz and gunfire was being exchanged in the heart of the city, by the Strypa River. On one side of the city were Russians; on the other, Germans. The people on the Russian side of the city, where I was, were the lucky ones. On the Russian side, one could move around freely, but on the German side, all the inhabitants were evacuated and relocated. The Germans had destroyed half of the city and killed any Jew who had come out of hiding.

It was April and extremely cold outside. I asked a Russian soldier if I could follow the retreating army and he agreed to allow it. There were many civilians among the retreating Soviets, and I spoke with a woman who was walking slowly and holding onto a wagon. I asked her if she was Jewish and she said that she was. Apparently, all or most of the civilians in the queue were Jewish; they had decided to go with the Russians if they could because they couldn't risk being controlled by Germans once again. They were understandably afraid that they would be killed.

There were approximately thirty people following the retreating army, and I asked the woman if she knew of other Jewish people still alive in Buczacz. "Not many," she responded, "but they had several good places to hide, so some stayed." I asked if she knew some of my family, and I gave her my surname. Unfortunately, she didn't know anyone and admitted that she was actually not from Buczacz. I later asked some other people in the row of Jews, but they also did not know my family, despite the fact that some of them were from Buczacz.

It was extremely difficult for me, but I approached Jasko to say goodbye. I had no mirror to see what I actually looked like, but I pictured myself as I saw Janek: a small, undernourished boy who was always hungry and who dressed in oversized rags. It seemed to me that returning to Jasko's home would be to return to a difficult but simple life. Jasko tried to convince me to stay with him until the war was completely over, but I declined his invitation. Now that I knew that most of the people who were walking with the Russians were Jews, I decided to go with them.

I didn't want to hide any more, and I didn't want to live the life that Jasko and Kaisa lived. I didn't want to look like a poor Polish boy or live in a one-room home. I wanted to be free and to live in a nice house and hopefully return to my previous quality of life. I had been frightened long enough. I didn't know what was going to happen to me, but I hoped that everything could be better than it had been. I thanked Jasko for always being so helpful and kind. He had fed me and taken care of me, and I knew that I would not have survived without him. He then told me that he had done it because he liked me, and that many times he wished that I had been his son. We said goodbye and I never saw Jasko again. I am very sorry about that. I would have very much liked to see him and Kasia, but circumstances did not allow it.

The retreating soldiers and civilians came under attack from the air. Stuka dive-bombers made screeching attacks on us, dropping bombs and strafing men and women as they scrambled to hide near the road. The planes were flying low, and bullets sprayed the area. Everyone fled into the fields, but the aircraft returned repeatedly. Dead bodies littered the road and nearby fields after several waves of attacks had ended. The army collected their soldiers — dead or alive — but picked up only wounded civilians, placing them in a wagon. I sat on the wagon next to a woman who had been wounded. She was obviously in pain and held my hand tightly. A few kilometres down the road, the convoy stopped near a school. The wounded — soldiers and civilians alike — were taken into the school in a suburb of Buczacz, which had been converted into a field hospital.

A big tent had been erected, and there were soldiers milling around. Food was being distributed to the soldiers from a field kitchen. I asked the soldier who was distributing food if I could eat as well, and he asked how old I was. I replied that I was fourteen years old and a Jew and that the Germans had killed my mother, father and entire family. By then, although I did not know for sure, I assumed I was alone. He asked if I had a canteen, and when I said no, he gave me his canteen and filled it with meat and soup. He gave me a large portion of bread and told me to sit in a corner, behind the kitchen, and said that he would talk to me later.

After he had finished serving meals, the soldier came over to me and said that he, too, was Jewish and that he would help me. He took me into the school and presented me to an officer. It was comfortably warm in the school. I had been almost frozen in the bitter cold outside. The soldier told the officer that I was Jewish and that my entire family had been murdered. The officer said that he had a boy my age at home, and he smiled. He then inspected me from head to toe. I knew that I did not look good in my shabby, torn, oversized coat, my shoes tied together with string and my hands red and raw from the cold. My face was definitely dirty, as I had not washed for months. I'm sure that my appearance was pathetic. He looked at me for a while in silence. He then told one of the soldiers that they had to clean me up, take me to the army stores and dress me properly, and be certain to throw out all my rags, as they were probably laden with lice.

I was taken into a room that was full of clothing. The soldier told me to undress and he gave me long underwear, socks, a pair of pants, a shirt, a *kufajka* (quilted coat), a hat with earflaps, gloves, a scarf and extra socks and underwear. He also provided me with a canteen, a fork and a spoon. I almost looked like a small soldier. He brought me back to the officer, who was pleased with the result. He said that I could stay with him for a few days, and then he would make a decision about what to do with me.

When he brought me to the home where he was staying, I will never forget how happy I felt. He gave me a bar of soap and told me to take a bath. I had not taken a bath for more than two years, and now there was hot water and soap! I could not believe that I was finally in a bathroom with hot water and white towels hanging on hooks. There was a mirror on the wall, and after the bath I looked at myself for the first time in years. I was clean and dressed like a little soldier and not like a "dirty Jew." What a monumental difference just a day could make in my life — the difference between hiding, afraid, in the woods, and then, in vivid contrast, being free and in this clean, bright bathroom with running hot water. With just a few hours of guidance from a helpful and friendly person, I was transformed from an animal into a human being.

I thought of Janek and was saddened, realizing that had he survived just a few more months, he would be here next to me, experiencing freedom and a full stomach. I thought that it might have been poor judgment on my part to go into the water to save the baby. If I had just listened to him and left the mother and child, he might be alive now. I felt that his death was my fault, and I felt guilty.

I remained with the Soviet forces for a few days, but the sounds of warfare continued. The friendly Russian officer told me that we were in danger: the front line was close and the Germans were still trying to advance. He arranged for me to ride in a truck convoy going to Czerniowce, Romania (present-day Chernivtsi, Ukraine), since there were many Jews in that city. He gave me some rubles and ordered the driver to take care of me.

There were six trucks in the convoy with two drivers per truck. They were going to pick up supplies in Czerniowce, and the drivers told me to sit in the front with them. It was only just over a hundred kilometres, but it felt like a very long ride, and I fell asleep. When they woke me, we were in the supply depot, and I spent the night there.

In the morning, the driver asked if I would like to come along for a ride into the city. He assured me that he knew his way around the area, and we drove into Czerniowce and stopped at the black market. This was a new experience for me. The driver removed a bag from the jeep and extracted a few items — a pair of military boots and a blanket — and exchanged them for bottles of vodka. He confided that this was not the first time that he had been involved in this kind of transaction. The buyer asked if I was the driver's son, and he said yes. I felt that it was so kind of him to reply that I was his son. I started to feel like I had value, like I belonged. At the supply depot, the driver asked me not to tell anyone about this exchange. At the same time, he told me that if I had anything to sell, this man was a fair buyer.

The next day, the trucks were loaded with supplies and they returned to the front lines. Before leaving, the driver told the officer in charge of the depot that he had certain orders; he gave him a letter and told the officer to let me sleep in the depot temporarily until I found a place to live. I could not thank that officer enough for his generosity and his help. I never saw him again.

When I was free, warm and not hungry, I thought of Jasko many times. If it had not been for Jasko, who had treated me like a son, I would not be alive. I was so thankful that he took care of me without getting paid. He did it from his heart; he wanted the best for me. I survived the war under Jasko's protection. He fed me with whatever little food he had, and he really did not have much. He shared everything with me. It was not as if he ate meat and gave me stale bread; his daily food was the same as mine. As I thought of Jasko, I knew how happy he would be for me if he could see me now, looking so clean and dressed so properly.

I remember thinking, Am I homesick for Jasko? I don't have anybody. Maybe I should go back to Jasko and live with him and his family. What if nobody from my family is alive? Maybe there is somebody left alive from my family? All these questions were going through my mind at once.

~

I was now free of the Germans, the Ukrainians and the war itself. I was in Czerniowce, Romania, the largest city I had ever seen. There were many tall buildings, paved streets, parks, a theatre and a large black market.

When I had heard that I was going to Czerniowce, I was very excited. I had two uncles on my mother's side living there. I remembered that one of the uncles visited my zadie, my grandfather, in Buczacz, and that one of his two daughters was my age. I now believed that I would be reunited with members of my family. I questioned many people at the market, but no one had heard of the Kissels. I then went to the city hall for a permit to live in Romania temporarily, and I inquired about the name Kissel. I did not remember many first names, but that proved to be unimportant. There were no Kissels listed in the municipal registries, as they had probably lived in the surrounding area. My excitement about becoming a member of a family again was short-lived. I never found any trace of the Kissels in Romania.

On the other hand, I loved the feel of a big city. I started to do some trading on the black market, just like the Russian soldier who brought me to Czerniowce, selling clothing for vodka, and then vodka for clothing! I even sold my own clothes and bought myself a suit, shoes, a shirt and a tie. I soon accumulated some money from black-market trading. In fact, I had done so well that I bought a gold ring with what I believe was an aquamarine stone, and I also bought myself a watch. I felt and looked prosperous. I always carried a bottle of vodka — not to drink, but to sell. I stayed in Czerniowce for about a year, and met many people through the black market where I was selling a variety of merchandise. At the time, the black market was similar to a huge department store and one could find almost anything that was wanted or needed: clothing, food, furniture, tools, weapons, books, cigarettes, real estate, sleeping accommodations, passports, smuggling connections, or even tickets to the opera or theatre. The black markets in Europe after the war were extremely important.

During the time I spent in the city, the war came to an end. By May 1945, Nazi Germany no longer existed. Adolf Hitler's "Thousand-Year Reich" had lasted only twelve years. Allied forces occupied a defeated Germany. In the Ukraine, the Russians had renewed their offensive and forced the Germans out of the city of Buczacz. It had taken months for the Russians to reoccupy Buczacz, and by July 21, 1944, the city was free of the Germans.

I feel that I made the right decision not to return to Jasko. I would have had to continue to live in rags and sleep in the stable, and who could predict what would have happened to me during that time. I didn't want to think about it. When the Russians reoccupied Buczacz, fewer than one hundred Buczacz Jews were left alive — and I was one of them.

By the time the war ended, more than sixty million people had perished — most of them civilians — including about six million Jews. More than 2 per cent of the world's population had been destroyed in a single conflict. Several hundred thousand European Jews had survived — some from Hitler's death camps and concentration camps, others from the Soviet Union, and a smaller group who had somehow escaped the Nazi killers and their collaborators. I was one of the few.

PART THREE
ON TO CANADA

Remember always that you have not only the right to be an individual; you have an obligation to be one. You cannot make any useful contribution in life unless you do this.

Eleanor Roosevelt

DREAMING OF ISRAEL

Most Jews who had survived the concentration camps or who had been in hiding were unable or unwilling to return to Eastern Europe because of post-war antisemitism and the destruction of their communities during the Holocaust. Many of those who did return feared for their lives. In Poland, for example, locals initiated several violent pogroms. The worst was the one in Kielce in 1946, in which forty-two Jews, all survivors of the Holocaust, were killed. These pogroms led to a significant second movement of Jewish refugees from Poland to the west, where they were housed in Displaced Persons camps and urban centres. The Allies, through the United Nations Relief and Rehabilitation Administration (UNRRA), established these camps in Allied-occupied Germany, Austria and Italy for refugees waiting to leave Europe. After the war, no countries wanted the Jews, and nobody was interested in their welfare.

While in Czerniowce, I met a young man by the name of Joe Schmerer. He had family in Bucharest — an aunt, an uncle and a brother — and he had a sister in Canada. My new friend Joe and I would talk about our futures and what we would do. He was older than me by about two years and suggested we go to Israel.

Arranging travel was extremely difficult because we were in Soviet-occupied territory. A permit was required to travel, and it was almost impossible to obtain one. The easiest way to travel in Soviet-occupied areas was to use military transport, as I had been doing, but all convoys were being checked.

To begin our journey to Israel, we would have to cross over into one of the areas controlled by the three Western powers — the United States, Britain and France. Above all, we needed to get to Bucharest, Romania, first. It was not difficult for us to travel because we had virtually nothing except the clothing on our backs, and the remaining small items could easily be put into a duffel bag.

I had gone to the army-supply depot where I had contacts. They were my most important supplier of merchandise, and in return, I provided them with vodka. I asked if they had a convoy going to Bucharest, and the officer said that he did. One was going to leave the next day, but there was only room to ride in the back of the truck with the supplies that they were transporting. I knew that we would experience an uncomfortable ride, but it was the best he could do at the time.

Joe and I had to make a decision immediately, and without hesitation, we decided to leave Czerniowce. We sold some of our items on the black market, concluded other business we were involved with, and then we were ready to go. We packed our duffle bag with clothing and bottles of vodka, which was more valuable than money. Vodka was extremely important to the Russian soldiers, so it could get us anything we needed. We turned up at the depot, and in return for two bottles of vodka, space was made for us on the truck, and we still had a few bottles of vodka left over.

It was, as I expected, a long, hard journey. The convoy stopped frequently to unload supplies. The entire five-hundred-kilometre trip took four days. In the evening, we achingly descended from the truck, stretching our legs, only to go back into the truck to sleep. When we finally reached Bucharest, the trucks were empty of their cargo. At the military camp where we had arrived, I approached an officer and asked if we could stay the night. A bottle of vodka sealed the deal. He took us to the mess hall, where there was a large number of soldiers.

The officer uncorked the bottle of vodka, and the Russians began to party — singing and dancing. One soldier played on his harmonica and others were dancing the *kozaczka*. I took out a second bottle of vodka — and then a third. The dancing and singing continued until the early morning. I think those bottles of vodka were the best investment I ever made. (The people I met that night became the principal suppliers and customers of my new business: vodka.) We were black marketeers and making money.

We stayed in Bucharest, Romania, for a long time, seven or eight months. We were getting comfortable, but we knew that if we wanted to get to Israel, we should begin our journey. We decided to get ready to leave for Budapest, Hungary. Travelling after the war was very difficult. Travel by train was complicated simply because so few trains were available, and there were no direct routes. There were actually not too many options. As long as we were on the Russian side, the best and most convenient option was to travel with the military, so I spoke to my contact at the Russian military camp about making arrangements to travel in their convoy. He told me that there were trucks leaving every day for Budapest, but I would have to "make arrangements" with the driver myself. Many soldiers knew who I was. They called me "the vodka kid," and the fee for accommodating two passengers was six bottles of vodka. It was not a bad deal for us, but it was actually a lot of money, considering the value of vodka on the black market.

That day, we climbed onto the truck and went under the tarp, which was covering their supplies for the overnight journey. In the morning, after an eight-hundred-kilometre trip, the driver let us off on the outskirts of Budapest. We walked into the city, not knowing a single person. We were streetwise now and simply asked for directions to the black market. These markets, although illegal, were lifelines for many people during this turbulent period in post-war Europe. It was while meandering through the market that one learned the latest news or where to find basics, such as a place to stay. It was here that displaced people like us earned a living by buying and sell-ing. Most of the transactions were illegal.

Once Joe and I had settled in, we took long walks through the city. We had established ourselves in the black market, and often we would relax in many of the sidewalk coffee houses. Joe was older than I was and looked more mature. Although I was a teenager now, I was really still a kid and looked like one. Yet I never considered myself a child. After all, I was totally self-sufficient.

Budapest was a very beautiful city located on the banks of the Danube River. On one side was Buda, and on the other, Pest; the cit-ies were combined, making Budapest. The streets of Budapest were paved with cobblestones, and at every corner there were restaurants serving great food. I remember paying ten US dollars for a dish of goose liver that was made especially for me. The goose liver was drowning in chicken fat and so delicious.

Joe and I looked for an apartment as soon as we reached the city, and almost immediately, Joe met a girl with a two-room apartment in the centre of the city. She was approximately twenty years older than Joe — but since I was only seventeen, everyone looked a lot older to me. She apparently liked Joe. I slept alone until I also found a girl-friend who was older than me.

We were doing very well financially, so well that I made a deal with a dentist who was living in our building. For a gold coin, he filed a perfectly good tooth of mine and capped it with a gold crown. At the time, this was considered a status symbol, although I removed the gold crown when I came to Canada.

We had a good income, but we had to contend with the unpre-dictable value of currency other than the American dollar. The value of the Hungarian pengo fluctuated wildly, and the government was printing money to pay its employees. So it was a wise decision to buy US dollars immediately after selling something. I realized that be-coming involved in the money market was more lucrative than sell-ing liquor. Primarily, this was because money was so easy to carry. I was catapulted into the currency-trading business when I wanted to buy a new pair of shoes. I had selected a pair of shoes, and the price was twenty-five million pengo, which was only twenty-five US dollars. I told the storekeeper to put them aside and that I would be back in half an hour with a friend and money. When I returned, the price of the shoes had risen to twenty-six million pengo — but it was still twenty-five US dollars. Obviously, the American greenback was the only stable currency in Hungary.

We stayed about eight months and then decided to move to Austria. Joe and I still wanted to go to Israel, even though Budapest was so beautiful. We were making money on the black market, and we both had girlfriends and had great connections, but we did not want to live in Hungary.

This was not an easy decision. Living well in a big city had been really exciting, and both of us now rented two-room apartments on Kazinczy Street. We even discussed whether we should open a store in Budapest and settle down, but Joe wanted to either join his sister in Canada or go to Israel.

Life in Budapest was wonderful, but of course, I thought of my family often. I considered returning to Buczacz to see for myself what had happened there. After all, the war was long over, and there were now no problems travelling around Europe. I still don't know exactly why I did not return. Perhaps it was because I knew that the trip would remind me of the horrors I had experienced there. I told myself that when I was older and settled, I would return, but never did I think of going back there to live. I did not want to live with daily memories of my murdered family. I had to start life over again and make a new beginning in a new country and escape the tragedies of war. Even while relaxing in my nice apartment, I could never forget the days when I was starving and hiding like an animal in the forest.

When I lived in the forest, I forgot what my life was like before. I was barely able to remember the days when I had slept in a warm, dry bed with white sheets and pillows. I was stuck in the forest with no future. It never entered my mind that my situation would ever change. I thought that I would live like that until I was found and killed.

The mind plays funny tricks on you when you are under such duress. As I said, the past fades away, and with it so many memories. The future holds no promise, only more of the same misery and unending days of hunger, cold, loneliness and fear. Not knowing whether you are safe or not is a slow form of torture. The sounds of the forest, which are so tranquil to me today, often sent me into a panic back then. The crack of a broken branch, the sounds of animals and the unfamiliar noises made me hold my breath and frightened me to the point where I could not even move. The words "they will find me and kill me" would play over and over in my head. I felt like the man who commits a crime and lives in constant fear of the day he will be caught. Except that I knew that when I was caught, death was inevitable because I was a Jew.

I would think of Jasko, the only person in my small world who helped me at a desperate time. I now compared my present life to his simple life. During my time in the forest I had no idea that I would live like this. My dream was only to be free and not live in fear.

Jasko was a good man. I wanted to write, to contact him, but did not have an address. I don't ever remember him receiving any mail in the years I was with him. I did not even know the name of the area where I was hiding. It was so remote that I don't think it had a name.

~

While business was good in the black market, our ultimate goal was to get to Palestine, the future Israel. On the other hand, if Joe's sister could arrange for him to get to Canada, the door might be opened for me to go there too. We still faced the challenge involved in reaching areas held by the Western Allies.

For information about how to get out of Hungary, which was under Soviet control, I approached the people in the black market.

They told me that we could hire smugglers to lead us, on foot, from Hungary into Austria, or we could try our luck with Russian truck drivers. There was a corridor used by Soviet truck convoys to drive from Hungary to Vienna, and there was no border inspection. We were told that if we travelled with smugglers across the border, we would not be able to carry anything, and we would have to sell what we had. But if we were to go by truck, we would be able to take our clothing and other items.

We decided to try our luck with Russian drivers. We packed our things and sold what was left to our contact at the black market. This contact had no US dollars, but he had watches and was willing to barter watches for our merchandise. We made a deal, and in exchange for our possessions, he gave us three watches and some Austrian schillings.

Joe and I took the train to the border, checked into a hotel and then found the military depot, where there were many Soviet army trucks and soldiers. I had learned Russian in school, so it was simple for me to speak to them. I asked how we could travel to Vienna. Some of the soldiers were going to Vienna the next day, and I made a deal with one of the drivers to transport both of us to Vienna in exchange for one watch.

Early the next morning, we arrived at the depot and immediately the soldier asked for the watch. I gave it to him quickly because he had already shifted boxes in the truck to make space for us and had put down a blanket so that we could sit or lie down. Apparently, this was not the first time that he had smuggled people across the border. We were well hidden, and the journey began.

After many hours of travelling, with many stops, the truck ground to a halt, and the driver told us that we were on the Russian side of Vienna. Wasting no time, we took a taxi to the black market, paying with the schillings we had traded for in Budapest. As usual, the market was the place to ask questions. We were told that if we wanted to go to Israel, we would have to cross over to the Allied side of the city and apply for a Displaced Persons card. With this card, we could travel to the territories occupied by the Western Allies: the United States, France and Britain.

The next challenge we had was how to leave the Soviet side and enter the Allied territory. At the black market, a merchant mentioned he had a friend, a taxi driver, who could drive us to the Allied side. He left, then promptly returned with the taxi driver, who responded that he charged twenty-five US dollars per person. We had been in Vienna for only an hour, but we boarded his taxi, and he drove us from the Soviet-occupied zone to the American side. Later I learned that it was very easy for taxicabs to drive across, and I realized that we had been tricked out of our money. Everything is a learning experience. The cab took us to the Bindermichl Displaced Persons camp, which was to be our home for months.

The DP camps in Austria held approximately 50,000 Jews. Many had survived forced labour or concentration camps, killing centres and death marches. Most did not want to stay in a Europe that was haunted by the Holocaust and were determined to start new lives on another continent. Other than to search for surviving family, Jews were especially reluctant to return to Poland because of the pogroms, as I mentioned. Many who returned found that others had stolen their homes and property. The chance of restitution was almost nil. Often, when they sought justice, they were murdered.

Most of the Jewish survivors wanted to go to Palestine. When the British government coldly refused to allow Jews entry and asked them for a second choice, they wrote down Palestine again.

Scores of Displaced Persons camps were set up, not only in Austria, but also in Germany, Italy and other European countries — sometimes in converted military camps. These were to be the homes of thousands of people for months before they were relocated. Everyone wanted to get settled and start a new life, but where would we go?

At the DP camp, we registered and received identity cards confirming we were Displaced Persons. This card gave us some important privileges. We could travel by train or city bus without paying. In the DP camp, we had a place to stay, receive food and make contacts, and we could leave and return as we pleased!

After settling in, we toured the camp and talked with many people. A large number wanted to go to Palestine, and we were told that one had to go to Italy for the chance to board a boat bound for Palestine. Meanwhile, Joe wrote to his sister in Canada frequently, and she would send him packages of clothing. On one occasion, he received a bag of potato chips. We had never seen them before and didn't know what to do with them. We tried cooking them, but they tasted awful. So we gave up on potato chips, at least for the time being.

When I arrived in Bindermichl, I found that there were no rooms available, and I really did not want to sleep on the floor or in the corridors. One section of the building had been bombed during the war, and there were no windows or doors left, but there was still a solid roof. I decided to clean out the debris, and I managed to find two windows and a door and install them, and in this way created a room of my own. Elsewhere in the DP camp, two families lived in one room.

The camp provided Joe and me with two beds, blankets, pillows, a small table, a small storage cabinet and other necessities. On the black market, we purchased a small electric stove, pots and pans, and an additional table and chair.

The people in the Bindermichl camp lived quite well and had plenty of good food. The local girls were eager to go out with people from the camp, as they could return home with certain treats, particularly chocolates and candy. I soon had a girlfriend who was Austrian, and not from the camp. Many of the girls we met were young and beautiful.

Joe and I started doing business on the Bindermichl black market, trading schillings for US dollars. Almost everyone wanted to go to Italy or Israel, and the best way to travel was to use US dollars. Banks were open, but there was a huge discrepancy when currency was exchanged. For example, in the bank, the exchange rate was ten schillings for one US dollar, but I could sell one US dollar on the black market for one hundred schillings — ten times the "legal" rate. The banks would not exchange money with civilians, only with soldiers, so people had to turn to black markets.

On some days, my pockets bulged with thousands of schillings. I suggested to Joe that we go to the Italian border and sell the schillings to American soldiers who were going to Austria. We took the train to the border and made a deal with the first American we encountered! We asked the driver if he needed schillings, and he said that he did, but he only had scrip. Scrip is the currency produced for US soldiers who are overseas, and is also known as MPC, Military Payment Certificates. US soldiers were paid with scrip because the US government did not want US currency circulating in Europe. They temporarily printed money that had the same value as an American dollar and could be exchanged for such in any legal institution. I then exchanged 3,500 schillings for 350 US dollars. The next day, I exchanged my last 2,000 schillings for 200 US dollars. In twenty-four hours, we had made 550 US dollars in profit! To celebrate our good fortune, we didn't bother with the train and took a taxi back to Bindermichl.

I soon entered into the currency-exchange business, and I hovered at the border between Italy and Austria, trading schillings for lira, much to my advantage. I became known as "the banker." When the Germans were retreating from Italy, some had robbed the Italian banks and then settled down in Austria. They transported millions of lira into Austria, but since they could not exchange lira in Austrian banks for schillings, the lira was virtually worthless on the Austrian side. They could only be sold privately or spent, and one would then have to cross the border back into Italy. There were no banking facilities within the camps, so I decided to fill the void. My customers were varied, and I sold them Austrian schillings for lira, at a considerable profit. I also acted as a money-changer for servicemen and others who were crossing the border.

One of my enterprises involved leading small groups of youths to

Zionist camps in Italy. While there was an organized effort to assist the young people, many more wanted to go, and I led dozens at a time, illegally, to the Austrian-Italian border at Udine.

~

I never really believed that Joe would leave me, but one day in 1947 he finally got his permit, visa and all the necessary documents to enter Canada, and it became a reality. He was very lucky that he had a sister living in Canada who enabled him to leave a depressed country where there was no hope and no future. All the dreams we had of going to Israel ended. I was alone again, having to start over and make a decision about what to do next. I was sincerely happy for Joe; he would be united with his sister, and he would be able to start a family. And I became a little jealous; I wanted the same for myself.

When Joe received the documents to immigrate to Canada, I asked him if his sister could also help me, perhaps posing as a cousin or some other relative. Joe was eager to help and suggested that I change my name from Oziac Fromm to Munio Schmerer. He was a cousin of Joe's who had been living in Czechoslovakia, and Joe had not heard from him. I was overjoyed by the idea that Joe and his sister might help me. Although the plan was questionable, and I didn't think it was definitely going to happen, I hurried to register myself as Munio Schmerer.

I did not know whether I would be admitted to Canada, so I considered other options. A group of *chalutzim*, pioneers, from Israel came to Bindermichl and asked if anyone wanted to immigrate to the Holy Land, and I was the first to volunteer. About twenty young boys were interested, and we went to the Italian border by train. We met a guide there who led us over the border on foot. On the Italian side, a truck was waiting for us.

Soldiers from the Jewish Brigade of the British army used their vehicles to transport Jews who were trying to get to Palestine. We were taken to the UNRRA camp at Udine, Italy, but the camp was not a comfortable place to stay. We were housed in an abandoned school, sleeping on mattresses adjacent to each other. Soldiers of the Jewish Brigade were bringing in more people every day.

At the time, I was reluctant to board a boat for Israel. I learned that if the Royal Navy intercepted our ship (and they intercepted most of them), we would end up in a camp on the island of Cyprus — behind barbed wire! Nevertheless, many took their chances. Thousands ended up in detention centres in Cyprus — to be freed only when Israel was born as an independent state in May 1948.

I continued to do well in Italy, exchanging currency. I purchased schillings from people arriving from Austria, paying one dollar for one hundred schillings. I travelled by cab to the border and back, to exchange schillings for dollars. I had a problem selling the scrip, so I would offer a 10 per cent premium while my competitors in the black market wanted 20 per cent for changing scrip to US dollars. No matter whom I dealt with, we always came to an agreement.

I wrote a letter to Joe asking him if his sister had made an application for me in Canada. I anxiously waited for an answer, and Joe replied, urging me to be patient, and saying that his sister was doing her best. I remained lifelong friends with Joe, and I considered him my cousin. His sister, Zofia, tried very hard to bring me over from Europe to Canada; I really appreciated everything Zofia did for me, and we always remained in touch.

But I still had nowhere to go. I was stranded in Italy and Joe had left for Canada. I was sad and lonely and had to make every decision by myself again.

No state, no country, no band of men can more truly be described as the linchpin of peace and world progress.

Winston Churchill (referring to Canada), 1930

CANADIAN REFUGE

Unfortunately, I received negative news from Montreal: I had been refused entry because the Canadian government did not consider cousins to be immediate family. At that time, the Canadian government did not want to allow in any Jewish refugees, especially into Quebec. I decided at this point that I would board a ship for Palestine because I realized that I had no one in Canada except Joe. I still had his last name, Schmerer, but I decided that when I arrived in pre-state Israel, I would change it back to Oziac Fromm, my birth name. I hoped it would be a better decision to go to Palestine, and that maybe I would even find some family there. I felt that, even though I was risking being interned on the island of Cyprus, Palestine was the only place for me to go. I was confident that I would eventually feel secure surrounded by my own people in Israel. I dreamed that if I ever reached Israel, I would join the Haganah — which in later years became the core of the Israel Defense Forces — and fight for the establishment of Israel.

One day, without warning, members of the Canadian Jewish Congress (CJC) came to the office at the camp where I was living and asked if there were any orphans under eighteen years old interested in going to Canada. They said that there were some families in Canada who were interested in adopting children, preferably aged four to seven. But the majority of those children had been killed in the

Holocaust. The ones who had survived were approximately twelve to fifteen years old because they had been able to take care of themselves. The members of the congress announced that any youth who were interested should come to the camp office and register but that the program was strictly for orphans.

I had had enough of Europe; I wanted to go to school or work and settle down and start a real life. I hoped that perhaps a nice family would adopt me. The representatives of the Canadian Jewish Congress told me that the Jews in Canada were anxious to help the orphans. I underwent an intensive examination, including a check on my health and tests of my reading ability in several different languages. If I passed the tests, they would advise me as to when to be ready to leave and what preparations would be made. Thankfully, I did pass the tests, and I was accepted as one of the one thousand orphans to immigrate to Canada.

I had three months to prepare myself to leave. This was a huge decision and a conflict for me. I was ready to go to Palestine, but I also wanted to go to Canada because Israel had not yet been created, and the only alternative was, as I mentioned, camps in Cyprus. I thought about how long I might be in a camp. Could it be a month, a year, ten years, my whole life? I had to make a decision without anyone's advice. I had to rely on myself. It was tempting to dream about being adopted by a nice Canadian family that would send me to school, dress, feed and guide me. I felt that my life could be better in Canada than in Israel, and I therefore decided to go to Canada.

I wanted to forget the past and forget all the horrors that I had experienced. I really did not want to remember. I wanted to start a new life. In Canada, I hoped that I could study art and become an artist. Everything seemed possible to me. I could go to school and educate myself.

However, Canada was not welcoming survivors with open arms. When I arrived, I learned that the CJC was having a difficult time settling the orphans. The government of Canada was not really working to help the Jewish refugees, even if they were children.

The door had opened to one thousand Jewish orphans, including myself, thanks to the efforts of Saul Hayes, the head of the Canadian Jewish Congress. Hayes was at the forefront of negotiations; in addition to convincing Ottawa to welcome the orphans, he went to each provincial government to seek a similar understanding. Every province had to agree to the arrangement.

Quebec premier Maurice Duplessis would not even agree to meet to discuss allowing Jewish orphans into Quebec. Hayes, a lawyer, then prepared a comprehensive document regarding his proposal, submitted it to Duplessis and added that if he received no answer, he would presume that the province had agreed to accept the young people. Instead, Hayes received word that the province would accept the orphans.

Hayes had convinced the Canadian government to accept the Jewish orphans, but all of us were subjected to an intensive screening process lasting as long as six months. The Canadian Jewish Congress would have to take responsibility for the orphans, as the Canadian government wasn't taking any responsibility — it was reluctantly opening the door slightly, but without enthusiasm. In the meantime, I and the other children were waiting impatiently to go to North America.

Those accepted — the final count was 1,123 — made the journey under escort, in small groups. Finally, in October 1948, my day came. A full month had passed before we were told that we would be leaving. Two military trucks came and transported us to the train station for the journey to Bremen, Germany. I was known as Munio Schmerer, and it was under this name that I was to be admitted to Canada. I wanted to change my name back to Oziac Fromm, but I did not want to rock the boat and ruin my acceptance into Canada.

The ship in which we crossed the ocean was not a luxury liner. It had been used to transport servicemen, and the orphans — all boys — found that tiers of bunks were provided for sleeping. Many were severely seasick; I, on the other hand, felt great and was happy. I became friends with many of the boys and we had a good time.

The ship, a US military transport called the *General Sturgis*, was at sea for a month before it delivered hundreds of orphans to Pier 21 in Halifax, where we were warmly greeted on the docks and given candy. There was a wide variety of languages being spoken. I could communicate in Polish, Ukrainian, German, Yiddish, Russian and Hungarian, and I later learned English and French. Eight languages!

Halifax was a city with a small but well-organized Jewish community, eager to greet the newcomers. Local businessman Noah Heinish greeted many Jewish immigrants to Halifax, and he gave me a five-dollar bill. When I received my Canadian five-dollar bill, I did not know its worth compared to the US dollar. In the train to Montreal from Halifax, I gave it as a tip to the waiter. Only later, when I started to work in the store with Joe, receiving eighteen dollars a week in salary, did I realize how much five dollars was worth.

The historic Pier 21 in Halifax, where I disembarked, looked like a huge prison. It had barred windows and cages for interviews. The reception committee was excited at the prospect of greeting and assisting young people who had survived the Holocaust. The volunteers welcomed us, conversing in Polish, Yiddish, Russian and German. With great difficulty, arrangements had been made for volunteer families to care for us, but would-be host families usually asked for "a girl aged seven or younger." Unfortunately, there were no little girls on our boat. As mentioned before, most of the orphans who came to Canada were teenagers, and the majority were boys. The Canadian Jewish Congress, obligated to find us homes and families, had run into great difficulties. The lack of enthusiasm among Jewish couples toward adopting or even sheltering an orphan shocked them.

On our arrival in Montreal, we were welcomed at a reception centre on Jeanne Mance Street, on the second floor of the Herzl medical dispensary. The social worker assigned to us was very friendly and spoke Yiddish. I was assigned to a room with another boy. Twenty to thirty young men were temporarily accommodated in the centre. We were visited by a number of families interested in adopting, and in some instances, they selected an orphan for adoption. Other children were assigned to foster homes and were escorted there by the social worker. The place was busy continuously.

The morning after we arrived, the social worker took some of us to a store to outfit us. The store, Schreter's, was located on Notre-Dame Street. It was already November and chilly, and we were provided with winter clothing. I was given a coat, boots, gloves and socks. In other words, I was outfitted from head to toe.

Joe visited and took me to meet his sister and uncle. When I arrived at his sister's home for dinner, I think they were all surprised at how well I was dressed. They made comments such as, "It must have cost a lot of money to dress you." I felt that, in their opinion, the social worker had spent too much money on me — in addition to the fact that the CJC had brought me to Canada. I was a newcomer, and people did not let me forget that.

I also received a negative welcome from some of the Jewish community. I remember taking a girl out one evening, and afterwards, she brought me home. The girl's father was blunt. He told me that they were Canadians, but the newcomers were taking all the well-paying jobs. He asked how it had been for me in Europe. I didn't really want to talk about the past, so I simply answered that it was bad. He told me that it was also bad in Canada because there was a shortage of sugar! I never saw her or her father again.

My early experiences in Canada, and those of many other young men and women, were not encouraging. I was assigned to a foster home. The family had two young girls. They were paid to provide me with a room — foster parents in Montreal were given forty dollars a month for children up to sixteen and fifty dollars for a youth over sixteen — and that is all they did. I was not allowed to wash my clothing in their house, and there were no meals for me, so I always ate in restaurants.

I had another experience underscoring the fact that I was a "newcomer." One of the girls had a boyfriend who was always around. The younger sister, who was slightly overweight, was not popular. Never-theless, I asked her out on a date, and she turned me down, declaring that she did not date newcomers. I knew that in their eyes I was noth-ing. Honestly, I did not blame them. The girls did not want to go out with me, which seems understandable from my perspective today as a parent.

Many people had no respect for me. After all, I was nobody, an or-phan. I had no family, no known background, no known history, and no way to prove anything I said. A few people thought that maybe I was not even Jewish. Even my name was not my real name. I felt like I was nobody, and no one wanted to get involved with me. I did not like it, but I think I understood. The Canadians made their feelings very clear to me. In Europe, I had been a Holocaust survivor — and not ashamed of it. In contrast, in Canada, I was never asked to tell the story of how I had survived because no one was interested. No matter what their status, almost everyone looked down on me, and it seemed that the poorer they were, the harsher the judgment. In those difficult first years, when I didn't have language skills, I was hungry for com-passion, for help, for friendship and especially for love.

I, among hundreds of other young people, had lost my entire fam-ily in the European bloodbath and hoped that Canadian Jews would open their homes and their hearts to us. Having lost my entire family and all my friends, I was hungry for acceptance into a new family. Instead, few families were receptive to bringing a young adult into their private world.

One day, my social worker advised me that a family was "very in-terested" in legally adopting me. I was picked up at the home where I was staying and driven to a home at Fairmount and Park Avenue. At the time, I did not realize that I had been staying in a more prosper-ous area, on Davaar Avenue in Outremont. The man drove me to the duplex where he lived, and we climbed the stairs to his apartment. His wife was playing cards when we walked in, and she paid absolutely no attention to me. She just continued playing cards. It was hardly the kind of warm greeting a prospective foster son would expect. My would-be foster father showed me what he did for a living. He took me down to the basement, where he had a printing press. He apparently printed business cards and invoices.

I would live upstairs, he explained, while I worked with him and learned the trade. He would treat me like a son, he said, and life with them would be wonderful. He said he would provide me with spending money, although no mention was made of a salary or an opportunity for education. We went back upstairs, where his wife was still playing cards and still showed no interest whatsoever in her new "son." I asked the man where I would sleep, and he explained that there were no actual sleeping accommodations for me, but there was a hide-a-bed in the parlour. He assured me that the parlour would be mine — six days a week. On the seventh, they needed to play cards there. By now it was about 11:00 p.m., and I was sitting in the kitchen alone. I got up and went outside. I knew the area as I had stayed nearby, on Jeanne Mance, when I arrived in Montreal. I needed to think. I felt that the man did not want to adopt a son and send him to school — what he wanted was somebody to work for him for free. Once more, I recognized that I was unimportant in their eyes and simply someone to exploit. To them, I would be a servant, but I did not plan to be anyone's servant. I had survived a war on my own. I walked back to the centre on Jeanne Mance and spent the night there.

The following day, the social worker asked me what had happened. The family was worried when I didn't return. I detailed what I had experienced, from the card-playing wife to the husband who was eager to have an unpaid apprentice. The social worker agreed with me that it seemed that they didn't want a son, just an unpaid worker.

I did not expect to be adopted as an actual son into a family. I only expected some kind of compassion, some kind of understanding of my needs. I was eager to go back to school and hopefully to art school, as the Nazis had robbed me of an education. There was a different plan for us child refugees. Many families decided that the orphans should go to work and that they didn't have to educate us; they had done enough by bringing us to Canada. It was true — they did rescue us and brought us to a beautiful, free country filled with opportunity — a country where a person can prosper, achieve and dream. When I consider the risks they took and the problems they had bringing us into Canada, I take off my hat to them.

This is how I think today. But at that time, as a young adult, I was not thinking of their efforts to save me. I wanted to retrieve my lost years; I wanted my childhood back. I wanted to be loved, and I wanted a family. But no one could give me what I wanted because that was destroyed in the Holocaust, and I could never get it back.

~

In Canada, I felt sheltered — free of the tragic experiences in Europe — but still very much alone. I was in my late teens and had no family, and virtually no one was concerned about what happened to me. My only friend, in a city of millions, was the young man I had met in Europe, Joe Schmerer. We worked together in the same store, where I had a salary of only eighteen dollars a week. It was ironic that before I came to Canada, I had been making much more money by wheeling and dealing on the black market. I assured myself that I would one day own a home, a car and a business, but in the meantime, I didn't know where to start. Perhaps, I thought, I could marry a Canadian girl, and then things might begin to improve.

I once met a butcher's daughter, and I will never forget that experience. She was short and not very good-looking, but her father owned a butcher shop in Outremont. He boasted that his shop was "the best in Montreal." He said he would pay me well if I worked in his store, and if I married his daughter, he would give me ten thousand dollars as a wedding gift. I gave some consideration to this idea. In the 1950s, ten thousand dollars was a lot of money, but when I visited the butcher shop and saw her father at work, covered in blood, I changed my mind, and I never saw the daughter again. I didn't want to become a butcher — I wanted to become a businessman or an artist. I wanted to be affluent, and more importantly, I wanted to be in love. I was only twenty years old, and my whole life was ahead of me.

I continued to work as a shipper with Joe on St. Laurent Boulevard, near Rachel Street. I was making twenty dollars a week now and paying twenty-five a month to rent a room on Jeanne Mance Street. The Canadian Jewish Congress saw that I was capable of supporting myself, and they felt that meant I was capable of being independent as well, so they waived their responsibility to care for me. I felt that because they had brought me to Canada, they were still partially responsible for my well-being. I still needed help adjusting to a new life in a new country. But they told me indirectly that the remainder of my life was up to me. Unfortunately, everything hinged on their budget. I was abandoned because I was making the bare minimum.

Did the CJC fail to provide enough assistance to orphans brought to Canada during the post-war period? I believe they did well while negotiating the arrangement allowing the orphans to be admitted into Canada, but the orphans needed continued assistance. After that, the CJC functioned simply as an adoption agency. When adopting a child, there is a responsibility for their well-being. It's necessary to provide an education, food, a safe environment and lessons in life. It is not sufficient to transport a child into a new country and abandon him because he is capable of making twenty dollars a week. Many of the orphans considered returning to Europe! One of my friends immigrated to Israel and became a member of a kibbutz. They gave him a home, provided him with an education and did not regard him as a newcomer, because everyone in Israel was a newcomer. I did not follow him, and I remained in Canada, alone but determined.

The room I rented on Jeanne Mance was in the same building where a nice family named the Safrans lived. I didn't like my room because it was under the steps. The Safrans had a bigger room available and would charge the same amount of money I was paying for the room under the steps, so I rented a room from them, and my life began to change for the better. The Safrans were also newcomers to Canada, and they didn't look down on me. They were actually interested in me. They wanted to know who I was; they wanted to know my background. They had also come from Poland originally but had survived the war in the Soviet Union, where they were living at the time. They were lucky.

The Safrans had a large extended family — aunts, uncles, cousins, nephews and grandparents — who had also survived the Holocaust. They had all fled the invading German army, retreating with Soviet military units into the Soviet Union. They had experienced a miserable and difficult time in the Soviet Union, but the most important thing was that they were not killed because they were Jews. They did not have gas chambers in the Soviet Union, and many families who fled there survived the war without loss. In some parts of the Soviet Union, the children went to school, the women maintained their homes and the men served in the armed forces. However, thousands of Jews living in the Soviet Union were sent to harsh labour camps in Siberia, where many died.

The loving Safran family included the parents, Srewl (Issie) and Masha, and two girls named Helen and Rhoda. Their father worked hard as a tailor to ensure that his children were educated. It is definitely beneficial having a father to guide you. I soon began dating Helen. She was going to high school at Baron Byng and spoke English quite well. I really liked her and was very happy to go out with her. She was very attractive and petite like my mother had been, and she worked and shared in the expenses of the household.

I was only a lodger, renting a room by the month, but this family invited me to have dinner with them many times. This was in sharp contrast to my earlier experiences, where I would be alone in my room and not be invited to share a meal with my foster parents. The CJC had been paying my foster parents for my room, but they had no compassion and did not see me as worthy enough to sit at the table with them.

I thought deeply about my future. I knew that I didn't want to continue to be a shipper forever, and I was constantly speculating about which direction to take to become a success, and was very determined to make that happen.

I later met an older boy who was a peddler. I considered peddling as a job, but being a peddler requires a car, so I bought my first car. It was very exciting, although I had no idea which vehicle would be best for me. Interestingly, I still don't know very much about cars. I went to a Ford dealership, where the salesman showed me a few cars, and I bought a Ford for $600. I made a $150 down payment and then I owned the car! I was ready to be a peddler. Since I didn't speak French very well, I decided to try my luck in the areas were English-speakers lived. I was told that the Eastern Townships were a good place to start. Farmers there paid cash most of the time, whereas in Montreal, people were more likely to buy on credit and make payments every week.

I saw that peddling could be profitable as I made considerably more money than when I worked as a shipper. I obtained merchandise on consignment and paid for it after it was sold. If it didn't sell, it could be returned. I earned decent money and became independent.

I opened a bank account, and I was happy, although I was not closer to my dream of painting and expressing myself through my art. I realized that most artists were poor, and I did not want that life, and since I was only twenty years old, I felt that I could let my dream of painting for a living rest for a while. I knew that I should concentrate on making a living, something I also enjoyed.

Nonetheless, I was eager to learn about art and thought that I might have talent, so I went to visit the Montreal Museum of Fine Arts. I was moved and impressed by the beautiful paintings that were hanging on the walls. In fact, I was overwhelmed. There were so many splendid paintings surrounding me, and I was inspired. My heart started to beat quickly. I wanted to paint, and I wanted to paint immediately. I decided to spend some time in the museum on weekends. The works of Kandinsky, Riopelle, Mousseau and many other artists impressed me. I was particularly inspired by abstract expressionism.

I asked Mr. Safran his opinion on painting for a living. He was a willing listener and interested in what I had to say about my artistic hopes and dreams. I told him that I wanted to be an artist, and he bluntly responded that art was not a profession and mentioned the expression "starving artist." He told me that most artists do not make enough money to support themselves and instead urged me to learn a trade. He told me that a trade would always guarantee a job. He continued by saying that he was a tailor and supporting a family. He was able to send his children to school, rent a house, and he planned, in the near future, to buy the house.

I knew that in my heart and soul I wanted to paint and that one day I would achieve this dream. Mr. Safran said that if I wanted to start a family, I needed a steady job and I needed to know that I would be paid every week and that I must live according to my means. He was realistic and sensible, and as I really didn't know what I wanted or needed, I decided to paint only as a hobby.

I had a natural talent for art but no academic knowledge, so I decided to go to the museum as often as I could. I also became a member of the YMHA (Young Men's Hebrew Association) and took lessons in art and sculpting. I loved the smell of oil paint and of being in a room surrounded by people with similar artistic interests. Everyone would be talking about how to prepare canvases and how to mix colours. I began to define my personal painting style. I bought several books from various artists, mainly abstract expressionists, in an effort to understand this particular school of art. I wanted to understand *why* I was attracted to abstract art.

Love does not consist in gazing at each other but in looking together in the same direction.

Antoine de Saint-Exupéry, 1939

UNION AND REUNION

I was on the lookout for a trade, as Mr. Safran had suggested. One of my friends worked as a furrier and was employed in a fur factory on St. Lawrence Boulevard, not very far from where I was living at the time. He told me to come in to the factory to meet an older man named Mr. Rivalis and to ask him for a job. Mr. Rivalis seemed to be a very nice man. He questioned me briefly, and then, even though I knew very little about fur, hired me to work as a blocker, someone who stretches fur. After a few weeks at my new job, I asked him to teach me how to sew fur using the sewing machine. He was reluctant and explained that he was afraid I would break too many of his needles. I offered to pay for the needles I broke, and he agreed to teach me. After about two weeks, I had become a decent fur operator since this was not my first experience using a sewing machine. I used to visit my grandfather's factory and sew for fun. I had benefited from the experience in my grandfather's clothing factory and now became involved in the fur industry.

Soon afterward, Mr. Rivalis increased my salary from eighteen dollars a week to twenty-five. It was not a large salary for me because, as a peddler, I sometimes made more than one hundred dollars a week. I was learning a trade, though, as Mr. Safran had suggested.

Meanwhile, as is my nature, I remained ambitious. There were many operators in the factory making forty to fifty dollars a week, even though I was as productive as they were. I approached Mr. Rivalis and said that I would like to be a cutter. At that time, a cutter was making between seventy-five and one hundred dollars a week, and if you knew how to cut mink, you were paid more than a hundred a week. I did not think that even Mr. Safran was earning that much. The cutters were manufacturing grey and black Persian-lamb coats, and Mr. Rivalis was not eager to see me cutting expensive furs. Breaking a few needles was much less serious than ruining a bundle of furs, he explained.

We made a deal. I gave Mr. Rivalis two hundred dollars, and he agreed to return my money if I was successful in cutting my first coat. Furthermore, he would still pay me only twenty-five dollars a week while I was learning to be a cutter. He led me to a large cutting table equipped with special knives and blades. He instructed the man working there, Manny, to show me how to use a pattern and cut the fur. I watched the cutter as he worked, and he did not mind. He explained that fur grows in one direction. When you lay down a coat, the direction of the fur has to be consistent: always downward from the collar, front, back and sleeves. The correct way to caress the skin was in the direction of the fur. I learned this on my first day. On the second day, I learned that the most beautiful skins must be placed on the front of the jacket, where they are most visible. I felt great after my two-day lesson. On the third day, I was cutting furs with the help of my instructor, Manny. I told Manny that I had given Mr. Rivalis a two-hundred-dollar deposit in case I ruined the bundle of fur, but Manny assured me that I would not damage the fur. He said, "Don't worry, you are a very determined boy; you want to be good in what you do."

I was very fortunate. Manny was older than me, probably forty, good-looking, tall and slim, and he liked me and was quite enthusiastic about teaching me. He was the second person, after Mr. Safran, who was interested in my history. As he taught me, I told him about my ordeal in Europe.

As I was standing at the cutting table, I thought of Mr. Safran. He was correct. Learning a trade was the right thing to do. I learned so much from Manny. I never knew his second name, and I don't think anyone did. He appeared to be the plant foreman, and was an experienced cutter of Persian lamb. Whenever a problem arose, everyone called him. We got along very well. I was the youngest cutter in the shop and was grateful that Mr. Rivalis liked me and had given me the opportunity to learn the trade. Manny was very impressed with my work and often told me that I was a natural in the fur trade and had a good eye. Occasionally, I laid out jackets better than he did, he admitted, but he warned me that Mr. Rivalis did not intend to pay me the full wages of a cutter, regardless of my skills.

After a month, I asked for a raise. Mr. Rivalis returned my deposit and increased my salary to fifty a week. I was making more money than many of the other operators now. While it appeared to be a huge increase, it was not the correct amount for a cutter of Persian lamb. However, I stayed on because I needed more experience.

Although I was doing quite well financially, I was not happy about my immediate circumstances. I didn't want to end up like Manny, standing at the same table, cutting lamb coats daily and routinely for the rest of my life. I often thought about Mr. Safran and his advice to learn a trade. I looked at Manny and thought of Mr. Safran, and both of their futures did not impress me. I wished that my future could be in art, but I remained with the fur company for another six months and met suppliers and customers. Then I started another chapter in my life.

I had made many good contacts in the fur business. One man, who was much older than I was, asked me to go into business with him and open a store on St. Hubert Street. His plan was to be a contractor for the fur trade and to manufacture fur coats. He wanted to work both sides of the trade, wholesale and retail. Unfortunately, he had no money, but I did. I had saved the profits from my black-market activities in Europe, my peddling and, most recently, from the fur business. He estimated that the cost of opening our shop would be one thousand dollars, and he was going to try to obtain two hundred of that from the Hebrew Free Loan Association. The association, founded in Montreal by Zigmund Fineberg, had helped thousands of refugees to start businesses, buy their first homes and send their children to university. The association did not charge any interest on loans, and they allowed one to two years to repay the loan on a weekly basis if you were employed. If you were not employed, you required a guarantor to co-sign. The available money was from donors and from the beneficiaries of the loans.

My prospective new partner suggested that Mr. Rivalis might sign a contract to conduct business with us. In any event, in 1950 we officially went into business as the Empress Fur Company, occupying a storefront in a new building on St. Hubert Street. Mr. Rivalis was very angry that I was quitting after he had helped to train me to work as a furrier, and he refused to do any business with us. Nevertheless, we opened our store and did quite well. Our staff included a blocker, an operator and a finisher. We provided a made-to-measure service for fur coats, and we stocked coats on consignment, paying for them only when they had been sold. We sold a wide variety of coats: mink, lamb, Persian black lamb, shearling jackets, stoles and coats for children. I started to travel regularly to Hamilton, Kitchener, Windsor, Toronto and Quebec City.

I now had a trade and my own business, so I decided it was time to get married, even though I was still very young, not yet twenty-one. I did not think of myself as young, though. I had never really felt young. While I strove to be successful, my deepest desire was to have a family of my own. I needed some sense of belonging, something that had been destroyed and taken away from me more than a decade before. I needed a sense of completion. I felt much older than I was and that time was running out. I was subconsciously afraid that something negative was going to happen to me. I had no patience. I still have no patience, and I do things impulsively. I make quick decisions in business and in my private life. I felt that if I didn't begin my family now, I might never be able to do it.

Living with the Safran family was extremely comfortable, and as I began dating Helen, I also fell in love with her; luckily, she felt the same way about me. We enjoyed each other's company immensely, so she stopped dating other boys and we started going steady. It was also very convenient because I was living in the Safran home. I almost felt like we were already married and living together.

In addition, and importantly, her father and mother were respectful and kind to me. Once, when I was very sick with a high fever, the family called a doctor, and Mrs. Safran took care of me and brought me homemade chicken soup, her specialty, a medicine for everything. I was, in essence, now enjoying family life. Every evening, when Mr. Safran came home, his wife always had dinner prepared. They would sit down as a family and talk at the table. They were a close-knit family, and they made me feel that I was part of it.

They lived in a large duplex that had four bedrooms — one of which was rented to me. My rent obviously helped pay the expenses. Mr. Safran was active in the Montreal Workmen's Circle and frequently went to meetings, and his wife frequently complained that he was spending too much time there.

With my fur business doing well, I felt that it was the right time to get married. I was certain that I could do even better in the future, and that it would not be a problem for me to support a wife. We would still live with the Safrans. Mrs. Safran behaved as if she was my mother, and I felt that she would take care of me as if I were her own.

Since coming to Canada, I had felt like an unwelcome immigrant, and I thought about changing my name from Munio Schmerer. I did not want to get married as a Schmerer. It was natural to change my first name from Munio to Max, so I decided to become Maxwell Smart, which sounded like a nice Canadian name. I decided that I did not want to rename myself Oziac Fromm because it reminded me of my past: my deceased family and the horrific memories of how they died. I felt that Oziac Fromm died with his family, and my new life had begun in Canada. I had wanted so desperately to forget the war, but now I realize that I made a huge mistake by not keeping my family name, and I very much regret it. When, at age eighty, I started to write this book about my life, it was in memory of my family.

On December 24, 1950, after receiving permission from the Canadian Jewish Congress, I married Helen Safran. At the time, the law required anyone under twenty-one to get parental consent to marry. As I had no parents, I had to go to the CJC, and they required seven guardians to sign documents before they could give me permission to marry.

I was incredibly happy. I now had a beautiful wife who loved me, and I was a member of a big family. I had a family, a wife, a business, a home and parents. Life was good.

One evening, while having dinner with my new family and addressing Helen's parents as I always did, "Mr. and Mrs. Safran," Mrs. Safran interrupted me and told me to call them Ma and Pa. Tears welled up in my eyes, and I no longer felt like an orphan. I had been alone for a very, very long time.

The Safran family was scattered across the United States and Canada. Mr. Safran's sister had come to Montreal before the war and had arranged for the family to immigrate to Canada. Helen's grandparents had immigrated to Los Angeles. There were numerous family members in New York who had arrived in the United States before the war. Many of them were quite prosperous, and they had helped Issie Safran to start his new life in Canada. A few years after Helen and I married, her sister, Rhoda, married a nice young man named Eddie Albert, and they eventually had two children, Alanna and Darren. I felt very fortunate to belong to a large, established family.

We were a young, happily married couple, and we were ready to buy a home. Helen worked as a secretary at a large company located in downtown Montreal. I had my own fur business, and we both worked hard. We had saved enough money to buy a home, have a baby and be a family. Helen said that her mother had suggested that we wait before having the responsibility of children. I knew that my mother-in-law was right, and I didn't regret waiting. Helen and I had a wonderful time. We travelled and were carefree.

Many houses were being erected in the suburbs, and there was a development that interested us not too far from Montreal, in the suburb of Chomedey. We had to cross a bridge to get to Chomedey, so it seemed like it was very far away. After seeing a model home, we became so excited; it was a beautiful and brand-new house with three bedrooms, a dining room, a kitchen, a living room and a garage. The new houses were situated on rough but levelled land, so there was no lawn with grass, there was just mud. I remember going to buy the grass and putting it down myself.

What really excited me about our new home was the unfinished basement because I would be able to set up a studio and start to paint. I had been looking for this opportunity since I came to Canada. Without consulting my father-in-law, I put down a deposit on the home. The year was 1957, and the address was 1740 Mayfield Avenue, Chomedey. I felt that it was quite an achievement for a Holocaust survivor to own his own home, and when we returned to the Safrans, we excitedly told them what we had done — but they were not very happy about not being consulted on such a big decision.

My life changed completely after we had moved to Chomedey. I began to paint on everything — jute, boards, cartons, dishtowels and paper. I also made my own canvases. I still have some of those early pieces, but they are not for sale.

In the 1960s, I started doing some figurative painting. I remember selling a small canvas depicting a clown to a man named Haim Radler. I had been buying electrical switches for my business from him, and when he saw this particular painting, he bought it immediately. However, I felt that I was not ready to present my work to the general public. Forty years later, after opening my own gallery, I met Radler's widow, Pnina, and she mentioned that she still had the clown painting hanging in her living room.

In the 1970s, I turned to Tachisme, which is an art form that had started in the 1950s. Tachisme is derived from the French word *tache* meaning "stain." I was also drawn to Dadaism because it rejected reason, logic and rationality. Unconsciously and consciously, my mind and my hands were being guided. The most interesting art form to me, however, was still abstract expressionism, also a post-war movement from the 1950s, which I adopted and refined into my own style. I became very interested in post-war artistic movements, and as I became more familiar with art and art history, I redefined my style and attitude. I was drawn to the style of Paul-Émile Borduas and Jean-Paul Riopelle, whose work had been displayed at the Montreal Museum of Fine Arts. I was also attracted to the paintings of Jackson Pollock, though my own style is considerably heavier, more dramatic and significantly more explosive. Another important influence in my pursuit of a unique style was Kandinsky. He was rebellious and refused to conform. He wanted to be free to paint his thoughts and ideas, and this was what I wanted as well. Of course, it would be up to the public to determine whether I had made my own unique contribution to the world of art.

Abstract art had become popular in America. It was a post–World War II art form and what was being painted was not realistic, but it was an event. It was the liberation from reality, politics and aesthetics. Many of the abstract expressionists used large canvases and painted them completely. The entire canvas was treated as being of equal importance, as opposed to only the centre, as was the case in most conventional artwork.

One of my first paintings was a very colourful abstract, a small piece approximately eighteen by twenty inches. When it had dried, even though it had not been framed yet, I kept it in my car and would display it to everyone at every opportunity. When I showed the painting to a man I did business with and he wanted to buy it, I felt so proud and so appreciated. It was quite an accomplishment to know that my art was worthwhile.

Over time, I developed my own style and people responded

positively to my work. I worked long hours and began to sell many paintings. The prices were reasonable, and I was thrilled that people appreciated what I created. It was very important to me to know that my paintings were being enjoyed and displayed in people's homes.

When someone asks me why I am an artist, I simply answer that I am compelled to create. I enjoy the act of drawing, painting and expressing myself, and losing myself in the task of creating.

~

In the years after we moved to Chomedey, many things changed. Chomedey became Laval, and Laval became a big city, and many young couples started buying homes there.

We furnished our home and had two children. Our first child, born in 1954, was a daughter we named Faigie, after my mother; and our son, Lorne, was born five years later. He was named after my father, Lieb. I felt happy and secure.

Time passes quickly when you are happy and satisfied. The children and Helen became my entire life. I became a father and provider, and I ensured that my children had the educational advantages that were denied to me by wartime circumstances. I also did my best to provide my children with the kind of parental guidance that is so important in a child's formative years: the guidance I did not have when my own mother and father were taken away from me.

I tried to forget about the murder of my family, but in my heart, they were always there. I tried not to think about them, but even after many years, their faces were etched in my memory. I would often think of how they might have looked now. During the many years that I had been living in Montreal, I had not heard of anyone from Buczacz. I belonged to the YMHA and had many friends from Hungary, Russia, Romania and Poland, but no one from Buczacz. It was as if the town had never existed. No matter how intently I searched for anyone from Buczacz, I was not successful.

There was a part of me that did not want to discover the details about the murder of my family. It was difficult enough trying to overcome the sadness and trying to forget the atrocities I had seen with my own eyes. I had been in Canada for so many years and wondered why no one in my family was looking for me. This simple and unfortunate fact underscored the reality that I had no one in the world. So, like many survivors, I preferred not to speak about the Holocaust with anyone. I did not want to remember the nightmarish years and how I survived. The war faded into a dim memory, and my world had begun anew in Montreal, Canada. Montreal was now my home. I had a business, a home, a wife and two children. The war had occurred a long time ago, and the memories were so unpleasant and hurtful. I did not want to talk about the past with my family. I only spoke to them about the future.

It was one day in 1964 that my father-in-law mentioned that he had gone to a new barber in the neighbourhood, and that the barber was originally from a town near Buczacz. Unfortunately, when my father-in-law asked about the name Fromm, the barber did not recognize it, but he told my father-in-law that he was soon going to Israel to visit his family and that there was a society there that helped find people and unite lost families. I gave my father-in-law a list of three names for the barber to try to find information on — Kissel, Klanfer and Fromm — as well as my phone number and address in Chomedey, should the society find someone from my family.

When the barber returned from Israel, he told my father-in-law that the society did not recognize any names on the list. But he said that they did record my information and promised to ask other members if they recognized the names.

A few months later, I received a letter from a woman in Israel asking why I would be interested in the family names Fromm, Kissel and Klanfer. She mentioned that she was related to these families and asked if I knew anyone from them. Of course, she was writing to Maxwell Smart, so she could not understand why someone named Smart would be interested in the Kissel, Fromm and Klanfer families.

I wrote back explaining the complicated story, and it turned out she was my auntie Erna!

We started to exchange letters, and I immediately began making arrangements to visit my auntie. I was overjoyed to finally find a member of my family. Now I felt that I had roots and family. Now I could verify my background. It was comforting to know that there was still someone alive from my past. I had so many unanswered questions, some of which were decades old.

I decided to visit my aunt and uncle in Israel with Helen, our daughter, Faigie, who was now ten years old, and our five-year-old son, Lorne. When my Auntie Erna and Uncle Jacob met us at the airport in Tel Aviv it was very emotional; everyone was crying and laughing and hugging and kissing. What a joyful reunion! It was a wonderful and memorable time for my family and me. We took a taxi to their home in Even Yehuda, and we reminisced endlessly about the past until the early morning hours. She asked why I hadn't returned to Buczacz, and I told her what Jasko had told me when he went to retrieve the money he was paid for keeping me. The restaurant owner had told him that there was no more money for him, as my aunt and uncle were dead.

My auntie recounted her experience with the restaurant owner when he came down that day to the group hiding in the basement. He had told them that the farmer came to his restaurant to let him know that I had been captured and killed. It was a double lie! The restaurateur had likely decided to fabricate this story in order to lessen the chances of the Nazis discovering his arrangements for sheltering six Jews. In his restaurant, frequented by people in the area, periodic visits by a peasant farmer must have been hard to explain. By lying to him, the owner of the restaurant may have felt that he was following the best strategy for ensuring the survival of the people he was hiding.

To us, it was not important to speculate too much about the past, although I did ask my aunt to help me locate Jasko. Unfortunately, my aunt had no idea where he had come from because the family who had brought me to Jasko had recommended him. For the most part, we didn't want to bring up all our lost years and all the pain. We were finally reunited.

My auntie and uncle lived in a small, prefabricated concrete home that had one bedroom, a kitchen and a bathroom. They had no guest room but had a small sitting area near the entrance. They had constructed a temporary bed using a few benches that were borrowed from a neighbour, and covered it with two mattresses, but it was not really suitable for the four of us. In any event, we did not sleep well that night. The children were lying between Helen and me, and I knew that it would be impossible to spend ten nights under these conditions. In the morning, I took a taxi to a Tel Aviv hotel and rented accommodations for both of our families. I wanted my auntie to stay with me in the hotel and enjoy herself. I remember that she would dress so nicely for breakfast, as breakfast in Israel is an important occasion, and she used to like to dress up. We went sightseeing, exchanged memories and ate dinner together every night.

A day before we left for Canada, I returned to my auntie's home because she had mentioned that she had something for me that had belonged to my mother. It was our magnificent, huge, sterling candelabrum, which had been a gift from my grandfather to my mother on her wedding day. Auntie Erna asked if I remembered it from my home, and I replied that I could remember that it was on the dining room table with candles lit at Shabbat dinner. I remembered Mother polishing it in the kitchen, and I pictured my entire house as it was thirty years ago. My mother had given the candelabrum to her sister to hide. My aunt had taken it into her bunker with her while she had been hiding for so many years. She had been hoping that one day someone from her sister's family might be alive and had a premonition that she should not sell it. Several times, when in financial difficulty, she had been offered a considerable amount of money for the candelabrum, but she refused to sell it. It is extremely old and very valuable. She was very happy that I could have it now and eventually bequeath it to my children. I will never forget when my auntie told me that since she did not have any children, she always loved me like a son. At this point, my aunt and uncle were in their seventies and still in love and taking care of each other. After hugging and kissing and promising to return to Israel, we left them and returned to Canada. I subsequently made many trips to Israel, and my auntie often visited us in Montreal.

The candelabrum is the most valuable possession in my home, not in monetary terms, but in symbolic value. It reminds me of my family and recalls the happy times spending Shabbat with them. The candelabrum feels like it is a connection between my mother and me, a connection that will last forever. I sometimes imagine that she is in my home, and often when I see the candelabrum, I reminisce about my previous life. I cannot explain my feelings rationally, but the candelabrum reconnected me with my family. If it had not been for my auntie, my past would have simply been a distant shadow in my mind.

I do not know where the many deceased members of my family are buried. The graves of relatives who had died long before the war began, long before the Holocaust, were also destroyed. I never wanted to go back to Poland, where there was nothing remaining to suggest that a Fromm/Kissel/Klanfer family ever existed. What did I have to go back to? It would have been too painful. The survival of my auntie and of the candelabrum — this magical piece of sterling — symbolizes to me all the generations before me and is of monumental importance to me.

Although my auntie and uncle are both gone now — my uncle passed away in 1976 and my auntie in 1988 — whenever I visit Israel, I light a candle at their graves. This is the only place in the world where I actually know that I have family.

Even a happy life cannot be without a measure of darkness, and the word "happy" would lose its meaning if it were not balanced by sadness.

Carl Jung, 1960

FINDING MY BALANCE

In 1965 I was operating a business that imported metalworking machinery from Japan and Taiwan, and the company's success resulted in a need for more space. I realized that it could be an opportunity for me to get into the real estate business. Several of my friends had begun purchasing property many years earlier and they seemed to be doing very well, so with this in mind, I decided to try to find a property to buy. I needed approximately 6,000 to 10,000 square feet of industrial space, and it had to have one or two large shipping doors to receive containers and be located in a central location with good exposure.

One day, while driving on Saint Urbain Street, I saw an industrial building for sale that was nestled among the duplexes and homes of the area. It was not exactly what I was looking for, but I felt that it had potential and decided to call the listing agent. The building was the right size for me, approximately twelve thousand square feet. The ground floor consisted of six thousand square feet of warehouse space, and there was office space on the second floor. Adjoining the building was a small piece of land that was approximately four thousand square feet. The building was currently leased to two tenants, but there was still enough vacant space for my business.

I had no knowledge of real estate as this was my first commercial real estate venture. I did not know to check with the city regarding

133

zoning, and the listing agent did not mention it. Subsequently, I found out that it was only zoned for residential use, and this unfortunate fact would cause me many headaches and much aggravation over the coming years. The agent mentioned that the building could be purchased for seventy-five thousand dollars, with a minimum deposit of ten thousand dollars, and that the owner was willing to provide me with a balance of sale. It sounded reasonable, and I had the ten thousand for the deposit without requiring a mortgage. Whether it was the excitement of owning a building or the need to take a chance, I felt my instincts guiding me.

When I got home and informed Helen, she said she wanted to see the building immediately. As we drove over, I hoped that she would not be disappointed, but I knew that it would be satisfactory for my business and hopefully a profitable investment as well. When she saw the building, she was actually very impressed and excited, and so was I.

At this moment, my past popped up like it always does, and I was thinking about myself only a very short time ago. I had been a nobody in Canada — an orphan, a boy without a family, without a mother, without a father and even without a name, a boy without supervision, a boy without guidance, alone in the world from the age of twelve. Do you remember the past? I asked myself. Yes, I said, I remember. I remember when I was hiding, when I was in the woods, alone in the cold, hungry, dirty, my only dream to have a slice of bread and to survive to the next day and not be killed. I remember clearly arguing with God because I had nobody to argue with, not even anyone to talk to, and feeling like I was going crazy. But this existence was in the past, I told myself, and look at yourself today; look to the future and look at your accomplishments after such a short time in Canada — you are married, you have your own family, you have two children, you are well-dressed, not in rags, you are not hungry, you own your own home, and now you are about to purchase your own building. I had thought that God had forsaken me, but he did not. There must be a reason he chose for me to live.

I don't yet know why, but what I do know is that out of about eight thousand Jews living in my city, only one hundred survived, and I am one of them. Thank you, I said to God.

I had had many encounters with the past over the years. In the two lives of mine, the past and the future are always there; they pop up very often, more now than before. I tried to keep them apart, but they are like two different people living in one body. The past is not welcomed in my future because the past is only hatred and misery, hunger and fear, not knowing what tomorrow will bring. No, the past is not welcome in my future. I want to forget but I cannot. I honestly believe that God chose for me to live, but he chose for me to live in the future and not in my horrible past. My past can never be part of my future because hatred does not blend well with happiness. Hatred kills, creates wars and incites racism; hatred creates antisemitism and genocides. Hatred created my past and this should never happen again.

~

Without any experience or advice from anyone, I followed my instinct and purchased the building. I had confidence that I would be able to solve any issues if they arose. My offer was accepted, and six weeks later I became an owner of my first piece of industrial real estate.

I moved my importing business shortly afterward and occupied part of the building for a few years. Business was going well, and I outgrew the premises and needed an even larger space. I sold 50 per cent of the Saint Urbain property to a plumbing company for seventy-five thousand dollars, more than doubling my investment.

Five years later, in 1973, I contacted the same agent to see if he had any other properties for sale. He mentioned that he had a prime piece of vacant land for sale on Wright Street in Ville Saint-Laurent, facing the Laurentian Autoroute. We surveyed the property, which had amazing exposure onto the highway, and I knew that this part of Ville Saint-Laurent was very sought-after. The land measured approximately 150,000 square feet and was currently a treed lot. It had industrial zoning for a 60,000-square-foot building, which meant that my business would occupy fifteen thousand square feet and I could lease out the balance. I instinctively liked the area and understood the potential it held, but I had no experience as a real-estate developer, and realized I would need a partner to undertake this huge project.

After a period of negotiation, I had an accepted offer and now had to proceed to the next step; I had to find a partner. I had several friends in the construction business, so I tried to decide who had the construction experience and courage to proceed with this industrious project. Building on spec is always risky. I considered partnering with my friend Eddie Stern, who was then successfully building homes in Repentigny. He had experience with construction, development and banking, and he was, like me, a decisive person.

I called Eddie, hoping that he would become my partner. The next day, we met in my office to discuss the project. We reviewed the offer together, and he too saw the great potential and the money to be made. Without hesitation, he took out his chequebook and wrote a cheque for half of the deposit, and we became partners. Eddie turned to me and said, "Now that we are partners, let me see what I just purchased." Very few people would buy a piece of land sight unseen. Through this gesture alone, I knew decision-making would be easy with Eddie. I knew I had found myself the right partner. This partnership lasted for twenty-five years. It was easy and fun to spend most of my business life with Eddie, and we both did well.

Over the next twelve months we cleared the land, prepared construction plans, got the necessary permits, designed the building and arranged financing. We were finally ready to build. Before long, the building was built, the empty space was leased to some excellent tenants and my machinery business moved into its new location.

This was the beginning of many real-estate projects I undertook with Eddie Stern. Over the next two decades we were able to accumulate a substantial portfolio of industrial and office properties for our business, Edma Investments, whose name was derived from "Ed" for Eddie and "Ma" for Max. Real estate was proving to be so lucrative that I decided to sell my machinery business and concentrate full time on real estate.

Eddie and I were not only partners but also good friends and neighbours. We both lived in Hampstead, and his wife, Shirley, was Helen's close friend. When Eddie and I started our partnership together, our children were little and in school. As the years passed, things changed, and our children grew up, completing their education and beginning their own careers. Eddie's sons, Derek and Richard, joined their father in his other company, Olymbec Construction, which eventually went on to become one of the largest privately owned real-estate companies in Quebec. My son, Lorne, went on to become a successful real-estate broker. After twenty-five years together, Eddie and I decided that we needed to go our separate ways. We terminated Edma Investments and divided the many properties we had acquired and developed. Eddie's portion of his properties merged into his Olymbec Construction and I opened a new company called Opex Real Estate Management. Sadly, Eddie passed away in 2012. I keep in touch with his wife, Shirley, and we have remained friends. I see Derek and Richard quite often, and my children deal with them on a regular basis. One day, Richard called, looking to buy one of my paintings for a birthday present for his wife, Marnie. He chose one of my floral paintings and said, "This one I know she will love." It made me very happy.

~

This happy and rewarding period of my life shuddered to a halt on December 24, 1984. Helen, my companion and my love, the mother of my children, died at the age of fifty-two, of cancer. It was a tragic and horrific loss for my children and for me. I was left alone again, as both of my children had their own homes. I was fifty-four years old and had learned, through terrifying experiences, that life continues whether you are devastated or happy.

My daughter, Faigie (Faith), had moved to Toronto. My son, Lorne, lived in his own home in Saint-Laurent. Faith married Ian Segal in 1986, moved to Ottawa from Toronto, and gave me two beautiful grandchildren — Tara and Jay. Lorne married Dr. Sharon Pearl, and they also have two wonderful children — Brandon and Adam. I'm grateful that they live close to me.

But at the time I was alone again, not a boy, but a fifty-four-year-old widower. I was not in hiding, but I was living alone, with memories of my wife, Helen, and the only sounds I heard in the big house were the radio or the television. I started to get depressed and feel sorry for myself. I began having nightmares about hiding in the woods, with no one to care for me. I had buried my past for more than thirty-four years, but frightening memories were tormenting me, and I could not bear to be alone.

Under the shadow of sorrow, I began neglecting my business and myself. I began to feel depressed and anxious. When the sun set and it became dark outside, I felt as if I was alone in the forest again, hiding from killers, and I reminisced about my absent and missed family. I felt all right during daylight hours, but the night brought back moments of terror. I did not know what to do, and I was lost again.

Helen's death had a psychological and physical effect on my life. She was so young when she died, but with all the medication and doctors available in Canada, no one could help her. It seemed that death had followed me to Canada. I was so crushed by the loss of my wife that I stopped painting completely. I was mourning so deeply that I ceased to do the one thing that I love to do — paint. I would try to begin a painting, and I would place a canvas on my easel, but I felt paralyzed. I was unable to create anything. My paintbrushes were dry, my easel was bare, and my business affairs were in disarray. Why me? I continuously questioned. Haven't I endured enough?

My children understood my depression. Once more, I was beset by demons that were welling up from the past. My fear of loneliness resurfaced. My home was merely a house in which I slept. Finding a companion to share one's life is a rare joy. What chance was there for me, once ravaged by the Holocaust and now scarred by the loss of my wife, to be happy once more?

I tried to plunge into my neglected business affairs to ease my pain. I knew that I would have to start my life again. Difficult as it was, I had to try to put my great loss behind me. I didn't know that a new chapter was about to begin, and my life would soon improve. I worked with a woman named Tina Russo, an attractive divorcee with a four-year-old son, Anthony. Tina was an administrative assistant in my office. One day, dispirited and tired of eating tasteless food alone, I asked Tina to go out for dinner with me. I was fed up with going home to a silent house, and I was attracted to this beautiful young lady.

Tina enchanted me. I asked her out again and again. The process of making my children understand that their father had been given a second chance at happiness began. Remarkably, within two to three years, Tina became a welcome, beloved member of the family, not only to my children but, remarkably, to my late wife's parents, the Safrans.

Tina and I grew as a couple, and I realized that she was an extraordinary woman. She had an impressive mind regarding business matters, yet she would rush home from work to cook my favourite food. Tina took a warm, maternal interest in Faith and Ian's infant daughter, Tara, when they visited, and Faith concluded that if Tina wanted to see her baby, she must be a caring and warm person. She made our gardens bloom with spectacular flowerbeds, which impressed everybody who passed the house. She inspired me to paint again. Many people from our neighbourhood enjoyed coming to our house to see the gardens that she had created.

Tina is an extraordinary individual and someone ideally suited to be my partner. I had found a treasured companion: a wife, a mother, a grandmother to my grandchildren and, as an impressive further dimension, a businesswoman and a spectacular gardener. Suddenly, my house in Hampstead came alive again, and I had a family once more.

When Tina came into my life, she had three brothers who were married with children of their own. Her eldest brother, Angelo, and his wife, Nina, have two sons named Marco and Louis. Her younger brother, Tony, and his wife, Mary, have two sons as well, David and Michael. Her youngest brother, Frankie, has a daughter named Amanda. Tina's parents passed away years ago, but she still has a close relationship with her father's sister, Auntie (Zia) Concettina Russo Monaco, in Santa Maria, Italy.

Tina and I blended our families to include my daughter, Faith, her husband, Ian, and their children, Tara and Jay; my son, Lorne, his wife, Sharon, and their sons, Brandon and Adam; and Anthony, Tina's son with her first husband, Peter Katsoudas. Tina became more than a companion; she inspired me with her presence. Unquestionably, Tina Russo Smart re-opened my world of happiness.

I felt, for the first time, able to recount the story of my horrifying experiences during the Holocaust. I was able to relive the nightmare of my early years. I had kept my past a secret for many years and never spoke of it. I did not want to remember because I would become depressed.

Most of all, Tina understood my need to paint. She had assumed most of the responsibilities of managing my real-estate business with quick-minded efficiency. When we are able to escape to our condo in Florida for a few weeks, I enjoy painting in one of the bedrooms that I converted into a studio. While in Florida, I paint almost every day, and when I have accumulated a large number of paintings, I send them back to Montreal. I sell my work privately in Florida, and some of my paintings were represented at the Sher Gallery in Gulf Stream. I paint in the living room as well, where I can work on oversized canvases. Tina is always happy to see me in my element. In the summer, I paint outside in our garden in Montreal while enjoying the fresh air. I began to sculpt recently, and Tina complains about the mess, but she actually does not mind very much.

A prominent Montreal auctioneer and art dealer, Abe Rogozinsky, of Empire Auctions, approached me and asked me to submit a painting to one of his sales. I was very excited because he sold art, was an art consultant and liked my work. My painting sold quickly at the auction, and he was very enthusiastic and asked that I provide him with three paintings per month for his auctions in Toronto, Montreal and Ottawa. When Mr. Rogozinsky saw one of my paintings in my home, he said that I was a "damn good artist." That particular painting is called *Heaven and Music #2* and it is a fairly large piece, 54.5 inches by 64.5 inches. I could have sold *Heaven and Music #2* many times, but Tina is enamoured with it.

Mr. Rogozinsky wanted to help to further establish my reputation as an artist. There was a new edition of *Guide Vallée* for the years 1993–1994 being printed. He decided to have my painting *Dreaming* (1973) documented in the book. At the time, I did not know very much about what the *Guide Vallée* was exactly, but I learned that it was a reference book presenting 1,570 artists and included their biographies and the recent prices their paintings were sold for. I was very honoured to be listed as one of the 1,570 artists, along with Jean-Paul Riopelle, whose paintings are valued at $800,000; Jean Paul Lemieux, with paintings valued at $100,000; Alfred Casson, with paintings valued at $65,000; and A.Y. Jackson, with a painting for $8,000. I was overjoyed to see my painting in print and was very satisfied with the price that Mr. Rogozinsky received at auction.

I was too occupied with my day-to-day business affairs to set aside time to meet the demand for my art! Finding the time to paint without interruption eluded me. I had to attend to business and, once more, postponed painting.

And yet, the canvases were accumulating in my three studios. Tina thought that I should exhibit my work because Empire had sold several and Mr. Rogozinsky was always asking for others. Tina suggested that I build a gallery in a 3,000 square-foot space in one of my buildings, call it Galerie d'Art Maxwell and have a grand opening.

I was enthralled by the idea. Other than selling privately and at Empire Auctions, I had not been promoting my work. I had been so proud that Mr. Rogozinsky had put my paintings in the same category as the Canadian masters. He said that he had confidence in my work, and his words reassured me.

Combining compassion with competence, Tina gradually assumed more and more business responsibilities, and this freed me to realize my long-delayed dream of having the freedom to paint. Our business is running smoothly, and I am free to spend time in my studios, doing what I love. Art and painting became my life, and I felt that I had to make up for lost time. I painted hundreds of canvases and sold many and donated all the proceeds to various charities.

Something in my psyche compels me to paint. So many years were lost, and I felt that I had to compensate for the stagnant periods in my life. I had to work harder to attain my goal of becoming a respected artist, albeit self-taught. I enjoy being surrounded by my paintings, and I love the smell of paint. I feel like I defied the odds and lived through hell, at a terrible cost, yet here I sit, in front of my easel. In a way, I feel that through my art, I have accomplished what Hitler and his killers wanted to destroy.

To understand the meaning of my painting is a difficult task. To explain this concept, think of a dream. You wake up not knowing what you saw or felt; yet you remember certain symbols, images and patterns. Throughout the day you ponder these symbols to come up with a concrete explanation. You have an idea of what it could be, but you never know for sure. And this is the beauty of my artwork.

Unknown

GALERIE D'ART MAXWELL

Gradually, the design of my gallery evolved, and in 2006 the Galerie d'Art Maxwell started to become a reality. A gallery of 3,500 square feet was designed, with eighteen-foot-high ceilings. A great deal had to be done before the spacious gallery could come alive with rows of works of art. I started to work with carpenters and painters in the gallery. We installed track and chain hanging systems from the ceilings, suited to the weight of my paintings.

We chose about 150 of my canvases for the opening show, as many as would fit on the walls yet maintain space for them to "breathe." Some of the pieces measured almost ten feet across and four feet high — for example, *Power and Victory*, an oblong vista. It bristles with black horizontals that reminded me of gun barrels. In it, explosions of red paint reflect the detonations that I saw shot into the road in front of me as we fled with the Soviets in 1944. In the forty-eight-inch by seventy-two-inch oil *Eclipse #6*, dusky orbs hurl around a fiery sun and worlds seem to be on a collision course. Many of the smaller canvases depict single vases of flowers, showing that beauty can emerge from destruction. They are placed according to Tina's expert eye.

When the space was completed, we carried the paintings downstairs from my studio on the top floor, which was an immense task. I needed someone to administer the gallery, and Tina was much too busy in our office; Tina's son, Anthony, anxious to get involved with my dream, helped to make the opening evening a huge success. Each painting had to be numbered, catalogued, named, priced and photographed by a professional, and one thousand catalogues had to be printed in colour. Invitations had to be designed as well. Anthony became invested in this intense undertaking, and everything was done to perfection. After months of hard work, the gallery was ready for a grand opening.

The invitations were sent, and Tina organized the catering. My fears arose. I worried that since I was a self-taught artist, what would happen to me if my work was not well received? This was not just a single painting that was being trotted out to admiring friends, but a major public show of my artistic development. What if only a few people responded to the nearly three hundred invitations that were sent? I prayed that the majority of these people would come to the gallery to see my paintings.

The important night arrived on September 27, 2006, and the crowds did not stop arriving. Friends, family, politicians, reporters, photographers, other artists and collectors of art all clustered around my work and commented with gestures of their wine glasses. In addition to those interested in art, a number of media people attended, including Ann Lang of CBC, Montreal, who had produced a documentary about me, and Heather Solomon, the long-time, highly-respected arts columnist for the *Canadian Jewish News*, who praised my work as being "electrifying." I could barely take it all in. Tina mingled with the crowd while supervising the serving staff and helping pose people for photographs, looking after every aspect of what had become my triumph.

Many who attended the opening purchased paintings. Some selected three or four canvases. As I recalled those bitter years hiding in the woods, it was unbelievable that the day had arrived when people who enjoyed and admired my art surrounded me. What an experience! Visitors were hugging and kissing me and congratulating me on the successful and memorable evening.

My children were incredibly proud of their father, the Holocaust survivor who was now being acknowledged as a successful artist. I donated four of my paintings to the dialysis department of the Jewish General Hospital for a program called "Art for Healing," headed by Mr. Earl Pinchuk.

Helen's spirit is always present; I decided to designate all profits from the sales of my work to the Segal Cancer Centre of the Jewish General Hospital in her memory. Tina and I presented the proceeds of the sale of the paintings, a cheque for seventy-five thousand dollars, to Alvin Segal, to be used for cancer research. The Jewish General hospital has since erected a plaque recognizing the donors. Tina and I feel that the gallery would be a beautiful venue to host other fundraisers for the community in the future.

The preface in the gallery's catalogue illustrates my story. I had kept my past a secret and never spoke of it except to those closest to me. The fact that my name changed frequently over the course of my life put another barrier between my past and my present. Now my past and present had merged, and I felt that my evolving identities were melding. As the guests embraced me and shook my hand, I heard a young voice in my mind echo, *My name is Oziac Fromm.* Then I said aloud, "Maxwell Smart."

PART FOUR
THE PAST
COMES ALIVE

THE DOCUMENTARY

I believe firmly in the call of "Never Again" that was heard at the end of World War II. Growing up in Poland and living through what I experienced, I knew how quickly and easily things could change, and I wanted to be involved in some way in preventing a tragedy like the Holocaust from happening again. In a world where racism, hate, xenophobia and genocide are just around the corner, we must remember and learn from the sins of the past. That's why I joined the Canadian Friends of Tel Aviv University. I liked the university's work in Holocaust studies and thought their annual reports on worldwide antisemitism and the state of Jewish affairs were a positive contribution toward making "Never Again" a reality. I felt their efforts were integral in helping to keep the status of Holocaust denial and incidents of antisemitism on the radar and on peoples' minds.

In 2018 the Canadian Friends of Tel Aviv University in Montreal chose me as their honoree. Aside from being part of their organization for many years, I was being recognized for my lifetime achievements as a Holocaust survivor. The earlier edition of this book, titled *Chaos to Canvas*, was just about to be published by the Azrieli Foundation, and my art was being featured in public and private collections across Canada. Over six hundred people attended the gala event, including friends, family and many dignitaries. Tina and I had met world-renowned scholar Dina Porat on one of our many trips to Israel. She was a professor of modern Jewish history at Tel Aviv University, head of the Kantor Center and chief historian at Yad Vashem. She travelled all the way from Israel to be the keynote speaker at the event. Other distinguished guests included the late Father John Walsh, Consul General of Israel David Levy, the Honorable Irwin Cotler, and past president of Tel Aviv University professor Joseph Klafter. This was one of the proudest moments of my life. This Holocaust survivor, this boy in the woods, was honoured by having such distinguished guests in attendance. What a difference from my past.

But even such a joyous and wonderful evening could not erase my past and the guilt that I continued to carry. My past was always there, it always popped up, it never left me. Six million Jews were murdered in the Holocaust. It was a disaster, but those six million had not died because of me. The death of my good friend Janek, however, was my doing. I had coerced him into the freezing water to save the baby, and because of this he fell ill and eventually died. I didn't intend for him to die, I only wanted to help a baby survive. So why did I still feel guilty?

Then out of the blue came Rebecca Snow, a young woman with a charming British accent. Rebecca, from Saloon Media, had been commissioned by the History Channel to make a television documentary on child survivors of the Holocaust. She had learned about my story from the Azrieli Foundation. I was in Florida when she asked to interview me. After taking some time to think about it, I invited Rebecca to come down to meet me and discuss the project. I was initially caught off-guard by the request and not certain I even wanted to learn about the film. When I was writing my book, I was nervous and depressed for weeks. The memories of all I had been through came to the surface. I was unfriendly and angry all the time, and I often had night terrors and had trouble sleeping. However, the more I thought about it, the more I realized it would be good to have my story recorded on video in a professional manner, to show the entire world the atrocities that had been committed during World War II. With all the world fixated on one screen or another, making the story accessible by TV, phone or tablet made a lot of sense. I recognized that young people might not take the time to pick up and read my book, but they might watch a one-hour video on their phone. Still, I did not really believe that such a project would get off the ground, let alone be produced and shown on major television networks.

I think it was Rebecca's enthusiasm and her seriousness about the film that finally convinced me to move ahead with the project. The day after I agreed to participate, Rebecca sent a car with a driver to pick Tina and me up and bring us to a studio in downtown Miami. The studio was set up to look like the 1940s and was equipped for the interview with more than six camera crew. I had been interviewed many times before, but this was by far the most impressive and professional setup. The interview lasted about four to five hours. Rebecca wanted to know everything about my life in the woods — where I hid, where I found food and even how I kept warm.

In the interview, Rebecca asked a lot of questions about Janek and the baby. She realized that I carried a lot of guilt about Janek's death as a result of saving the baby. Rebecca said she wanted to see if she could get enough information from me to try and trace any records of Janek or perhaps find out what had happened to the baby. If she had survived, would that somehow alleviate my guilt?

Would it really make a difference knowing what had happened to her? Nothing could be done now. Janek was gone. The baby was probably long dead. I had so little information; I didn't know Janek's full name or even the baby's first name. Over the years, I had spent a lot of time and effort looking for records of my own family. I was desperate to find some living relatives, to somehow find a picture of my mother and father that I could look at. I knew their names, yet still I could find nothing. Maybe Rebecca and her team of researchers would be more successful.

At the end of the interview Rebecca showed me a black-and-white photograph of a young boy taken some time before the war. She asked me if I recognized him. I wasn't sure . . . but there was something about the eyes. She prompted me: "Could it be Janek?" Her research team had found an entry in the Shoah Names Database, a phenomenal project run by Yad Vashem whose goal was to name every single one of the six million Jews killed during the Holocaust. The entry in the database was for a ten-year-old boy named Janek Arenburg, who had been reported murdered by the Nazis in the area near Buczacz in 1943. I stared at the picture of the healthy, well-dressed, happy little boy. "It could be him," I said. I did recognize the eyes. He didn't look like that when I knew him — the photo had been taken before the war — but yes, it could be him. I asked to keep the photograph and I couldn't stop looking at it. Those eyes would haunt me until the next filming experience with the crew.

The first interview took place in February 2019. A couple of months later I received a call from Rebecca telling me she would like to continue filming the documentary. She also told me that her team was doing a lot of research and the next interview would take place in Israel. I knew the project was on a tight budget, and flying Tina and me to Israel was a big expense, so I asked why they couldn't film the interview in Montreal. Then Rebecca told me she had good news: the filming had to be Israel because after two months of arduous research, they had located an aunt and an uncle of Janek living there. I could not believe what I was hearing. My heart started to beat fast, and I felt as though I was going to explode. Rebecca continued talking, telling me she had uncovered even more information. Her research team had connected with Yahad-In-Unum, an organization that searches for mass graves and execution sites in Europe. They believed they had found the site on Fedor Hill in Buczacz where my parents and my sister were buried, along with 3,000 others, in a mass grave. Using a metal detector, they had found artifacts belonging to the victims lying in the forest: a pocket mirror, a button, a cufflink.

And the evidence of the perpetrators was everywhere — the ground was littered with World-War-II shell cartridges. I was dumbfounded and could not speak.

I knew I could never bring myself to return to Buczacz. But what about Rebecca's offer to fly to Israel? I had never dreamt I would have the opportunity to meet Janek's family and tell them in person what he had done to save the baby. Tina, who is a very spiritual person, considered this whole turn of events to be a message from God. After a few days to recover from Rebecca's revelation, I called her back and told her that I would go to Israel to meet Janek's family.

JANEK

After a long and tiring trip, we arrived in Tel Aviv, Israel, on a typical warm, sunny May day and checked into the Hilton Hotel on the ocean. The seven-hour time difference made me feel even more nervous and exhausted. I started to wonder if I had made the right decision. I was afraid of what was to come. What would happen when I met Janek's family? What would I say? What would they say? Would I be alright? Could I take this kind of excitement? I was scared and very nervous about this meeting. At Tina's suggestion, we took an extra day to rest and visit my auntie and uncle's graves in Even Yehuda cemetery. This also gave me an extra day to calm down.

Even Yehuda cemetery is a main destination for me when I'm in Israel. It is a place where I can go to be with my extended family. My immediate family is buried in mass graves in forests with no markers, an area that has been forgotten and plowed over. If I had felt that I was able to return, I would have said a prayer for my mother, my father and my sister on Fedor Hill. There are so many graves that have been forgotten in Buczacz. Out of the 8,000 Jews who lived there, not one is alive today. Such a great injustice was committed.

When Tina and I returned from Even Yehuda cemetery after visiting my aunt and uncle, I told her to make arrangements to see Rebecca and continue the interview for the film. Rebecca had set up a very professional-looking interview area in one of the large conference rooms at the hotel. As her crew was busy setting up the cameras and the lighting, Rebecca informed me that they had chosen a name for the documentary: Cheating Hitler. The name was a reference to me and the two other survivors who were to be featured in the documentary, all of us young children at the time, who were able to foil Hitler's plan to exterminate every last Jew in Europe.

At one point before the interview started, the head researcher for the documentary, Natasza Nedielska, walked in and Rebecca introduced us. Natasza explained that she searched the Ukrainian archives to find out more about my early life, but there was no information available as so many records had been destroyed in the war. Natasza did not give up easily. She then contacted archivists in Warsaw, since Buczacz had been part of Poland before the war. It was there, in the Warsaw archives, that she found my parents' marriage certificate. Natasza handed me a visibly old document, a hand-written marriage certificate that was almost one hundred years old. I was really surprised, as I had not expected to learn anything new about my family. A shiver went through my body and for a second I had no idea what she was showing me or saying to me. I was dumbfounded. It took me a while to digest what I was hearing and compose myself. This was the first concrete evidence of my mother and father I had seen in over seventy-five years. I took the piece of paper. I wanted to hold it in my hands. I wanted to feel it. This certificate, which was signed by my mother and my father, was the closest I had been to my parents since they were brutally murdered so many years ago. It included the date and place where they were born, the date of their marriage and the names of my grandparents on both sides of my family. It was a heart-stopping moment for me. Today, this certificate is one of my most cherished possessions. When I returned home from Israel I had it framed, and it hangs in my home office, where I see it daily and feel my parents' presence with me at all times.

All of this new and overwhelming information, along with the knowledge that I would be seeing Janek's family the next day, was very stressful for me. I wanted a day to rest, but Rebecca was prepared for the visit to Janek's family, so we had to go. Tina and I were picked up at noon, along with a cameraman who would be filming the visit to Janek's family's home.

The house where Janek's family lived was nestled in a garden with beautiful flowers. As I left the car and started walking toward the home of Janek's family, all the memories of Janek and me alone in the bunker came flooding back into my mind. Janek's auntie had survived the Holocaust by using false Aryan identification documents. She met us at the door and introduced me to her daughter, Miri, and her husband, Shimon Shirfris, the youngest brother of Janek's mother. He had left Europe for Israel before the war and had received letters from his sister back in Poland until the German occupation in 1942.

There was a table set up with refreshments for Tina and me. We were treated like royalty. Janek's auntie and uncle showed us their very comfortable home, filled with shelves of books and a piano in one corner. After we had had some refreshments, Janek's auntie came and sat across from me. Taking my hand, she said, "I am so glad that you are here to tell us about Janek. You know more about him than we do. Please tell us how you met. How did he come to you? Please tell us." She only remembered him as a small boy, maybe five years old. She showed me a picture of him, and as I stared once again into those haunting eyes, I started to talk.

"Janek found me," I explained. I told her what had happened to my family and how I had ended up in the woods. I talked about how I had found a bunker in the woods and the dangers that were everywhere. I told Janek's auntie about the loneliness that had haunted me every single day until the day I peeked out and saw a small boy walking alone in the woods. I told the auntie that he had looked better-dressed than I did. He had shoes on his feet and I had only rags tied with string. I explained how Janek had started to cry when he told me that he thought his mother and father were dead.

The family listened to every word I said and did not interrupt me. I kept looking at the picture that Janek's auntie had shown me. The Janek I remembered was a little bit older and skinnier than the boy in the photo, but I realized they were the same person. I explained how we had survived in the woods, looking for mushrooms and berries in the summer, learning to tell the difference between which mushrooms were poisonous and which ones were safe to eat. Life with Janek was relatively good. We suffered separately but quietly and did not complain. We told each other stories about what we would do the day we returned to our homes and our families. We didn't let the horrible truth of our reality have an impact on our dreams for the future — we needed to keep hope alive to survive. As I was talking, Janek's auntie was crying and so was I.

Finally, I arrived at that fateful day. I explained how early one morning, Janek and I heard shooting not too far away. I told her how it was winter and it had snowed all night, so we had to be cautious not to leave tracks in the snow. I said we had waited a few hours after it was quiet and we assumed the killers were probably gone.

Janek's auntie told me that when they heard nothing from Janek's parents after the war, they assumed the family had either been killed in mass shootings, like so many Jews in eastern Poland, or deported to concentration camps and exterminated. They had no idea Janek had survived in the woods for so long. She asked me how he had died. And so I told her the story of the baby. I couldn't help but break down as I told her about the guilt I still felt for pulling Janek into the cold water to help me save the baby. I felt responsible for his subsequent sickness and death. As I finished telling her about Janek's death, she took my face in her hands and told me not to think that way. She told me it wasn't my fault. Janek's auntie said that I had given him food and friendship, and that I had helped him when he was lost and alone. In reality, I knew he had done the same for me.

I had felt guilty about Janek's death for years, but now his auntie was telling me, with tears in her eyes, that there was nothing to forgive. She said I had had no choice but to go into the freezing water to save the baby. I started to cry again. I was so happy to be with Janek's family and to be able to fill in the missing pieces of his short life for them. We were both crying, but this time we were crying tears of happiness. Her forgiveness and understanding meant more to me than words can say. It was a moment that I will never forget.

TOVA

inding Janek's family was not the only part of my past that was being researched for the documentary. Rebecca told me that Natasza had also been trying for months to locate the baby that Janek and I had rescued. I had spoken to Natasza on the phone from Montreal and given her as much detail as I could about the area where I was hiding, and everything I could remember about the group of people who had been in hiding with the baby and who had been massacred. Natasza had spent months poring over survivor testimonies and historical maps, and digging up post-war records on Jewish orphans who fit the profile of the baby. Her list was long, she told me.

Then just a few days before I flew to Israel, she had come across another testimony that fit my story almost exactly. This survivor, named Tova Barkai, was living in Haifa. Natasza believed that Tova was the baby Janek and I had saved. I was completely overwhelmed. My whole life I had blamed myself and the baby for Janek's death. But if the baby was alive it meant that Janek had not died in vain. This made him a hero. He had given his life for hers; he had given her the gift of a long life. I was so happy and excited. This was the baby for whom I had almost been killed. As I was looking for someone to help me, or someone who could take the baby, I had been caught by the Ukrainian police, who dragged me with my hands tied to a sleigh for miles. Janek and I really had saved her life. Thanks to Natasza's hard work and diligence, I now knew that Janek had not died because of my actions. Janek had died because he saved the baby.

The day after meeting Janek's family, we left for Haifa. As we were driving, I kept repeating to myself that I was going to see Tova, the baby. I don't know if I really understood in my mind who she was — I had spent most of my life thinking about the baby that Janek and I had saved from certain death, not thinking about her grown up and living her life. All my life I had blamed myself for Janek's death because of this baby we had saved. It was unimaginable to me that the baby was alive, and yet here I was driving in a car to meet her! The baby was alive, and she had a family, children and grandchildren. Janek had not died for nothing. He was a hero. Both of us were heroes. Without Janek and me, she would have definitely died. We had given her life. She was here today because of Janek and me.

We arrived at the nursing home where Tova lived. Rebecca's camera crew were waiting in the lobby along with Tova's son, Ofer, his wife and their two daughters. I was warmly greeted by Tova's family. They served us drinks that they had prepared, and Ofer brought out a family photo album to share with us as we sat and got acquainted. Ofer explained that his mother had been sick for some time, so he had brought the pictures for me to see what she was like when she was young and healthy. The photos showed a beautiful woman in her early-to-mid-30s who looked happy. As I turned the pages of the album, looking at snapshots of Tova's life, I could not help but feel satisfaction and immense pride for this baby that Janek and I had saved. We had given her life, we had given her this beautiful family. In the blink of an eye, I saw Janek and the baby and a life saved.

As we were talking, Ofer told me that his mother didn't know about Janek and me. Tova's auntie, the woman I had handed Tova to back in 1943, had raised her after the war and told her that she had rescued her from her dead mother's arms on the riverbank the morning after the massacre. The auntie had written me and Janek out of the story. Perhaps she felt guilty because she had promised to return and take us back to her bunker, but never did. Times were very difficult, and she couldn't help us. I understood that the auntie had had a hard time with the baby. Hiding with a baby was extremely difficult and very dangerous. There was probably no extra space for Janek and me in the bunker, so I do not blame her for not coming back for us. I was happy that they had survived and Tova was alive. Even if Tova wasn't aware of it, I knew that Janek and I had saved her from certain death.

Ofer explained that his mother had Alzheimer's. As a result, she was unable to talk or move, and she had been in the same position for a year now. I heard Tova before I saw her as Ofer wheeled her into the room where we were gathered. She was crouched in her chair like nothing existed in the world. I went over close to her and said, "It is me, Tova. I know you don't remember me because you were a baby. I went into the freezing water with Janek and saved you. It was me. I am here. I survived. Janek, my friend, did not. He got sick. I lost my friend, the only friend I had. I was so scared to be alone, Tova. I wanted to die too. I wanted to be with him." I was so involved with my memories, I did not know if I was thinking these words in my head or speaking them out loud. I felt Janek next to me as I spoke to Tova.

"I survived," I repeated. "It is me, Tova. Janek did not survive. Janek died." Think hard. Think. Think harder. I knew I was repeating myself. I started speaking in Yiddish, the language of my childhood. I asked her several times to look at me. The cameraman was bent over on the floor, filming and recording what I was saying. Suddenly, Tova raised her head. Her eyes were wide open and glazed as if she was tearing up. She stretched out her hand to reach mine. She squeezed my hand and caressed it as she started to talk. I did not understand a word she said, but it sounded like she was repeating the same words I was saying. She was trying so hard to say something to me. She did not let go of my hand. Tears started to roll down my cheeks as I kept talking.

"Janek and I went into the cold water, we did not know you were in the arms of your mother. I saw a movement from across the river;

I thought that your mother was alive. I told Janek that we had to help her. On our side of the river all seven people from the bunker were dead, including your father. They were lying in the blood-soaked snow. I grabbed Janek's hand and we had to go across the river to save your mother. He did not want to go in. It was cold. He was afraid to go into the cold water, but I did not listen and pulled him into the water anyway. Our bodies became numb. I reached your mother, Tova, and she was dead. You were alive. You were the one who had moved. It was you I saw from across the river. I pulled you away from the arms of your dead mother. Tova, I am so sorry. I left your mother half-immersed in the freezing water and half-lying on the edge of the river, covered in snow. I am so sorry, Tova. I did not know what to do. I could not move her. I could not bring her over to the other side. I could not stay in the water too long. I had you in my arms. I had to run back to the other side. I am so sorry I had to leave her there. I could not do anything for her. I returned to the other side with only you and Janek. I only saved you. I brought you into the bunker your father had built. You were crying so loudly."

Tova continued struggling making sounds until words started to come together, and finally she said to me, "Everything will be good. It's okay." Her son interrupted me, overwhelmed because she hadn't spoken in over a year. The crew was filming and recording this miracle. Tova was correct: everything was good and it was okay.

After an incredibly fulfilling day, we said an emotional goodbye to Tova and her family. This was yet another experience that words simply cannot capture.

REFLECTIONS

The emotional impact of meeting the families of Janek and Tova was very powerful and had a profound effect on me. I could not rest. The conversations from that day were always on my mind, and those meetings were the only subject discussed in my home for many months.

I stayed in contact with Tova's family. It meant a lot to me that she had survived, built a family and created joy and happiness in her life. She had survived the Holocaust and the war without any idea of the horrors that were unfolding around her at the time. She went to school, got married and had children and grandchildren. I was happy when I looked at the pictures Ofer had shown me of his mother in her younger and better years.

But for me personally, it was different. As I reflected on my life, I realized that even though I was trying to move forward I was constantly reliving the past and the part that Janek had played. My memories had little to do with Tova. Yes, we did rescue her from certain death — I know she would have frozen to death by morning — and I am happy that we did, no question about it. But there was a cost.

Who is Janek to me? Janek is a hero. A life was taken in exchange for a life that was given. I am happy that this burden, this guilt I have carried my whole life, is no more. I really do think that what happened in the woods was a miracle. Janek and I needed to meet, to be in that spot at that moment in time, to put ourselves in grave danger in order to rescue Tova from inevitable death. I have no idea what made me so determined to go into the freezing water; it must have been some kind of instinct that required Janek and me to do the right thing. It was a miracle!

AFTERWORD

Born in 1930 and raised in Buczacz, Oziac Fromm became Maxwell Smart some years after he came to Canada in 1948 as an eighteen-year-old refugee. "I felt that Oziac Fromm died with his family," Maxwell explains. Already called "Munio" by friends in post-war Vienna, the name easily translated to Max. "Smart" was the moniker given by a Montreal acquaintance who admired his business acumen. Indeed, Maxwell Smart's story is not only one of miraculous survival, courage and ingenuity, it is also an account of post-war resourcefulness, return to community and enduring creativity.

Buczacz today is a town of 12,500 inhabitants in Ternopil *oblast* (province), southwest Ukraine. Like many towns in Eastern Europe, where borders were re-aligned during wars and after victories, its national status has shifted — at various times part of Poland, Austro-Hungary or the Soviet Union.[1] Until World War II, the town's mixed population reflected this political record. As 60 per cent of the town's pre-war residents, Buczacz's Jews had a lengthy and successful history. Among their distinguished native sons are Emanuel Ringelblum

---

1   For a comprehensive and detailed history of the town, see Omer Bartov, *Anatomy of a Genocide: The Life and Death of a Town Called Buczacz* (New York: Simon & Schuster, 2018).

(1900–1944), historian and compiler of Oneg Shabbat, the hidden chronicle of the Warsaw ghetto; Simon Wiesenthal (1908–2005), Nazi hunter and founder of the Vienna Wiesenthal Institute for Holocaust Studies; and Israeli writer and 1966 Nobel Prize winner Shmuel Yosef Agnon (1888–1970), whose stories "Buczacz: The Epic Life of One Town," "The Tale of the Menorah" and "Pisces" depict the town as a model of a successful Polish and Jewish community.[2] These men are modern heroes: one who left, making *aliyah* to Jerusalem, and two who faced the Nazi terror and preserved records of that catastrophic time. In "Buczacz," Agnon's story of the town's origins, a group of Jews making their way to Jerusalem receives permission to spend the winter in the town, where they camp out in their impermanent Sukkah huts. When invited by local landowner Count Potocki to manage his estates, they postpone their departure and remain in Buczacz, prospering until the Nazi expulsions and murders. Agnon describes their success:

Little by little the entire place came to be settled by Jews. They built themselves a ritual bath and whatever else community needs.... Even the noblemen and their retainers would come there for advice or business, knowing they would find Jews there. The place acquired a reputation; people began to come from far and wide, knowing they would find Jews there.[3]

In Buczacz, with its medieval castle and the Strypa River flowing through, the Fromm family led a comfortable bourgeois existence. Oziac's father, Lieb Fromm, owned a men's clothing store; Oziac's mother, Faige, was from a large prominent family; and his cousins were his playmates. Home was comfortable and welcoming, and the

---

2 See S.Y. Agnon, "Buczacz," in *A Book That Was Lost and Other Stories*, ed. Alan Mintz and Anne Golomb Hoffman (New York: Schocken Books, 1995), pp. 220–226. The title "The Epic Life of One Town" has also been translated as "The City Whole."

3 Agnon, "Buczacz," p. 225.

synagogue was a site for celebration and community. Young Oziac did well in school; one teacher singled out and praised his drawing of a book, which, for many years, was the only image he made. Oziac enjoyed the pleasures — and certainties — of small-town life.

Even after the town came under Soviet control in 1939, life for Oziac continued with relatively little disruption. But this all changed in 1941, when German forces beat back the Soviets and occupied all of Poland. Buczacz was further occupied by Ukrainian forces who were sympathetic to the Nazis and deeply hostile to Jews. In his detailed history of Buczacz, historian Omer Bartov describes the ceaseless antisemitic pillaging and murders of those years. The record is mixed: some non-Jewish residents sheltered Jews, but as atrocities multiplied, it became clear that, in general, Ukrainian residents were willing allies and accomplices of the Nazis. For Jews in Buczacz, Bartov writes, "instances of unadulterated goodness appeared miraculous precisely because of their rarity."[4] The town's shifting national history produced, in Bartov's account, "a complexity of rescue and betrayal," with Poles hating Ukrainians, and Ukrainians hating Russians and aligning with Germans, sharing the hatred of Jews.[5]

In *The Boy in the Woods*, Maxwell recounts his experience of narrowly escaping deportation and living at the edge of death for two years. He is helped by a young, poor Polish farm couple, Jasko and Kasia Rudnicki, but like many Polish rescuers, they are watched by their neighbours, and so send the boy into the nearby forest for long stretches. There, although alone and fearful, he also finds a sense of cosmic place, even order, as the night sky becomes a space of refuge and certainty. "I imagined I was travelling in space and time," he writes. "I would dream and detach myself from reality.... It was almost relaxing to gaze at the sky, the treetops and the birds.... How wonderful it must be to be a bird, flying around freely...." Decades

---

4 Bartov, *Anatomy of a Genocide*, p. 257.
5 Ibid., p. 254.

later, this cosmos he inhabited as a child would be the main subject of his art.

Unaware of other Jews hiding in the forest, Oziac's human contact is sporadic — limited to secret visits to Jasko's farm and brief interludes with other wandering Jews. It is hard not to read this in biblical terms: an expulsion from the Garden of Eden, a struggle to survive in the wilderness, the search for company, and the awakening of new skills and capacities. Chapter by chapter, we come to know the teller of the tale — his thoughts, his fears, his loneliness, his will to survive — although by a certain point in the story, he is so alone that the reader has forgotten his birth name. In his isolation, the boy doubts and derides his Jewish identity, angrily lamenting his fate to God. "Why was I a Jew?" he asks. "If I wasn't Jewish, I would not have to live in constant fear.... Why was my God not taking care of me?"

After the war, the search for renewal and a new home presents a forking road of possibilities: Palestine or Canada? Oziac — now called Munio Schmerer — eventually rejects the uncertainties of Palestine, which is still under the British Mandate and refusing entry to Jews. Munio's post-war adventures involve three years of movement and inventive financial schemes in Europe,[6] his immigration to Canada and a new life in Montreal. With the help of the JIAS (Jewish Immigrant Aid Society), in 1948 he comes to Canada on the *General Sturgis,* is welcomed at Pier 21 by members of Halifax's Jewish community and settles in Montreal. He is eighteen years old.

The Canadian part of the saga has its own difficulties and surprises. Canada's post-war immigration policy was complex, and in retrospect, clearly ambivalent. One government directive of February 1946 declared that refugee resettlement "would be based on national status." But, as historian Franklin Bialystok points out, "since Jews were not a 'nation,' they were without status."[7] Jewish refugees

---

6   For a compelling novel about post-Holocaust survival and opportunity, see Melvin Jules Bukiet's *After* (New York: Picador, 1997).

7   Franklin Bialystok, *Delayed Impact: The Holocaust and the Canadian Jewish Community* (Montreal & Kingston: McGill-Queens University Press, 2000), pp. 43–46.

were admitted to Canada through the efforts of the Canadian Jewish Congress, the agency then directed by Montreal lawyer Saul Hayes and the JIAS.[8] The process was not simple. A "workers' project" allowed approximately 3,000 Jews skilled in carpentry or needle-trades to enter the country with their families. After considerable lobbying, the federal government grudgingly agreed to admit 1,000 orphaned Jewish refugees; 1,123 arrived.[9]

Maxwell's (then still Munio) account of his first months in Montreal and the ambivalent welcome the young refugees received is a discomforting history.[10] Some in the Jewish community — most of whom had come to Canada in pre-war decades seeking refuge and a better life — disdained the newcomers, seeing them as threats to their own livelihood and sense of well-being. Their status as Canadian citizens and British subjects, many believed, was still somewhat fragile, and a significant rise in their number or any government attention was often unwanted. This was especially the case in Quebec, where provincial and civic authorities — long dominated by the antisemitic sentiments of the Catholic church — were not always sympathetic. For some Jewish Canadians, the post-war refugees, many of whom

---

Bialystok's study is a detailed account of the resistance and difficulties that the refugees faced.

8 For more on Hayes's important role in advocacy for Canadian Jews, see *Delayed Impact*, pp. 70–72.

9 For further accounts of this history, see Ben Lappin, *The Redeemed Children: The Story of the Rescue of War Orphans by the Jewish Community of Canada* (Toronto: University of Toronto Press, 1963); Irving Abella and Harold Troper, "One Wailing Cry," chap. 7 in *None Is Too Many: Canada and the Jews of Europe, 1933–1948* (Toronto: Lester Publishing Limited, 1983, 1991), pp. 190–237; Bialystok, *Delayed Impact*, p. 48; and Adara Goldberg, *Holocaust Survivors in Canada: Exclusion, Inclusion, Transformation, 1947–1955* (Winnipeg: University of Manitoba Press, 2015), especially chap. 2, "Ordinary Survivors," pp. 43–74. For a recent account of these difficulties, see Michael Fraiman, "A Fresh Start: The Story of Canada's Postwar Jewish Orphans," *Canadian Jewish News*, March 28, 2018.

10 Bialystok, *Delayed Impact*, pp. 63–67, and Goldberg, "The War Orphans Project," *Holocaust Survivors*, pp. 75–101.

were well-educated and skilled, seemed like an influx of burdensome "poor cousins."

Maxwell's experience was not unusual for post-war immigrants; it also touched Canadian-born Jews like me, a young girl growing up in Montreal's post-war neighbourhood, Snowdon. The area housed mainly young families, mostly English-speaking, and many — but not all — of them Jewish. Filled with the energy of post-war renewal and opportunity, the area (possibly comparable to the Levittowns in the United States) brought a proudly modern and acculturated out-look to a young adult generation of Canadian-born Jews. We were synagogue members, I went to Hebrew school three times a week, our kitchen was kosher and we celebrated all the holidays. The Jewish General Hospital was a few blocks away, as was the new Young Men's Hebrew Association (YMHA).

Modern, energetic, optimistic about our lives and our Canadian future, we were eager to leave the tragedies of Jewish Europe behind. Our future, many believed, was Westmount, Canada's richest com-munity. We disparaged our less-acculturated brethren on the east side of Montreal's Mount Royal. "Delayed pioneers," we called them, or worse, "mockies," an old Jewish slur.[11] This was, I believe, not un-usual in a multicultural country where ethnic homogeneity was rap-idly becoming ethnic pluralism and what we have come to describe as a national mosaic rather than a melting pot. It did not take long for me, as a student at McGill University (where there was not yet a department of Jewish Studies) and a young adult, to realize how acculturation's ideals could impoverish my identity, experience and understanding of history.

Maxwell overcame Montreal's initial disappointments. In 1950, not yet twenty-one, he married Helen Safran, and with astound-ing inventiveness, became a successful business and family man. "I

---

11 The term was at times used by more-assimilated Jews to label — and mock — newer or more old-fashioned immigrants.

opened a bank account," he writes, "and I was happy, although I was not closer to my dream of painting and expressing myself through my art." After several years, he returned to the artistic skills of his childhood.

Maxwell's art developed and flourished in Canada, a progression of a skill that began in primary school when his teacher praised the first-grader's drawing of a book. The war short-circuited any further development. But perhaps the boy's skill with his hands, his eye for shape and structure and his grasp of materials not only signalled early talent, but also fuelled an ability, even a confidence, to understand the spaces and structures of his changing environment and to survive. He built hiding spaces in his family's flat, and he dug out and "furnished" cave-like hideouts in the woods. Most importantly, he found comfort — visual comfort — staring at the night sky, as if the cosmos was a constant realm of promise, beyond good and evil, perhaps even returning his gaze.

The trigger that returned Maxwell to his childhood dream of being an artist was a junk-store find. Rummaging through a Craig Street pawnshop, he was attracted to — and bought — a painting of a landscape. Such things are usually sold for their frames, not their artistry. And to be sure, the pawnshop painting was not a lost masterpiece. But the picture re-awakened Maxwell's desire to recover his youthful talent. He revived an almost-forgotten ambition and set another goal: to make art.

The project included study at Montreal's Saidye Bronfman Centre for the Arts. For forty years, from 1967 to 2007, "the Saidye" offered classes in a range of visual media — painting and sculpture, as well as photography, jewellery and design — taught by a diverse group of art professionals and specialists. While it was hardly the only art school in the city, for students of all ages the centre provided a uniquely multicultural learning environment.[12]

---

12 The visual arts program at the Saidye Bronfman Centre closed in 2007. Some explanation for the closure can be found here: http://www.cbc.ca/news/entertainment /new-focus-on-performance-means-closure-of-saidye-bronfman-gallery-art-school -1.571075.

Memories of life in hiding shape Maxwell's art in both content and style. Underscoring his loneliness, the images show no figures. Whether realist or abstract, the images are unpeopled; like the artist, the viewer is alone. A group of undated drawings describe the house and country surroundings of Jasko and Kasia Rudnicki's farm. One image centres on a barn and waterwheel on the far side of a stream; other picturesque cottages rise along the hillside slope (pg. 40). The viewer is able to scan the landscape, but the water keeps us separate from the rustic scene. Other drawings come closer to a farmhouse, but again full access is denied. The cottage and barn appear as closed and shuttered structures; another drawing shows the log-roofed house nestled in the winter woods, but a roadway crossing the foreground acts as both frame and barrier, turning a welcoming vision into inaccessible refuge.

In contrast, Oziac's hiding place in the forest seems welcoming. The sketch of the bunker (pg. 61) is an interior view, seen from innermost space, as if the viewer shared the spare but cozy refuge. Light pours in through a small, arched entry, and a small stack of firewood is set along one wall opposite a modest covered tub. Upright logs support a wood-slatted ceiling from which hangs Kasia's old pot, whose holes allowed it to function as a makeshift charcoal heater. As a prominent object in the design, it hangs in tandem with the entry below. The scene is rather hospitable: remembered and drawn as a safe enclosure from danger or death, and an ironic contrast with the vision of the inaccessible farmhouse.

Learning his craft also led Maxwell to Montreal's Museum of Fine Arts, where on repeated visits, he found inspiration and artistic company in the works of Jean-Paul Riopelle (1923–2002) and Paul-Émile Borduas (1905–1960), Quebec's leading abstract expressionists. The turn to abstraction was not exactly new. Paris in the 1910s and 1920s attracted artists like the Spanish Juan Gris (1887–1927), the Dutch Piet Mondrian (1872–1944) and others whose canvases were based on gestural or geometric forms, with little or no recognizable imagery.

There are, to be sure, glimpses of shapes and figures in these designs, as well as a sense of atmosphere, but their impact depends mainly on colour, shape and the force of their overall design. In a modern world that seemed too turbulent or uncertain for realistic representation, the energies conveyed by paint and gesture expressed a new, existential state of mind. In Riopelle's *Gravity* (1956, MMFA)[13], for example, brick-red slabs fall and pile across the foreground, but equally, they rise through the grey-blue and white matrix and make their way to, and beyond, the picture's upper edge. And in Borduas's *The Flowering Crannies* (1953, MMFA), a floating cluster of colour is punctuated by slabs of white, scattered like blossoms through a green and brown milieu. The slabs of paint in the centre of Riopelle's and Borduas's large canvases evoke both landscape and cosmic configurations that hover in space and mind.

Recalling young Oziac's comfort in the night sky, we may understand Maxwell's attraction to Riopelle's and Borduas's abstract pictures. Maxwell draws a distinction: "My own style," he writes, "is considerably heavier, more dramatic and significantly more explosive." Indeed, the primary image in Maxwell's art is the direct opposite of his country-refuge drawings. Painted rather than drawn, the cosmos — for it is more than simply sky — became his recurrent subject and continued his youthful and solitary dialogue with God.

Small or large, his pictures seem to be segments of an immeasurable universe or a vast earthly space. What determines their energy — and every picture pulsates — are strokes or daubs of colour. Maxwell paints with a palette knife, not a brush. Each mark is clearly part of a pattern, but there are no firm contours or edges. Colour and the shifting directions of the strokes evoke an environment or atmosphere. But unlike the painters he admired, whose designs are invariably

---

13 See the work at https://theartstack.com/artist/jean-paul-riopelle/artwork-1923 -2002-1956-gravi.

centred and suspended in space, Maxwell's abstract imagery is filled with a coursing, directional energy.

Despite its soothing title, *Dreaming* (1973) affirms the artist's own description of his "explosive" style. Clusters of white lines burst through a turbulent matrix of blue, green and pungent red. And though the white "event" or presence is prominent against the darker tones, the entire canvas — figures and ground — pops and leaps with the energy. *Composition in Green* (1975) [Number 198] is a more lyrical example. At four feet by seven feet, the horizontal canvas suggests a panorama, or a portion of one, that extends infinitely beyond the frame. Or perhaps we look down into some fathomless depth. Slim diagonals of white brushstrokes blown to the left or marching to the right move in a procession across the field of paint. As always, they evoke some location in nature, and in this work, regularity and calm. The images are charged with energy. Unlike the centred forms of a Borduas or a Riopelle, they are expansive—even surgin —without a fixed origin or terminal point. Infinitely variable, this style has lasted through the decades since Maxwell began painting.

There have been setbacks and tragedies. Helen died in 1984, and for the first time in his life, perhaps, Maxwell was truly able to mourn. He struggled with a debilitating depression, and the past returned to him. He describes its terrors eloquently:

I began having nightmares about hiding in the woods, with no one to care for me.... I felt as if I were alone in the forest again, hiding from killers, and I reminisced about my absent and missed family.... It seemed that death had followed me to Canada.

In 1994, Maxwell married Tina Russo, who had emigrated from Italy as a child and settled in Montreal. Tina has boundless faith in her husband's art practice and a strong business sense, and now manages their real estate firm. Maxwell paints. His work is on permanent exhibit, curated by Tina, in their Galerie d'Art Maxwell.

In recent years, a quiet domesticity has entered Maxwell's visual repertoire. Inspired by Tina's garden, Maxwell has found new subject matter to paint: flowers in a vase — roses, tulips, chrysanthemums — stand centred in a vertical frame, beckoning to the viewer, greeting us and inviting us into their space (see, for example, *Joie de Vivre No. 3* [2004]. It seems, at first, a startling shift: these friendly bouquets appear to be the polar opposite of the abstract pictures' celestial energy and turbulence. They do, however, make a fitting if unexpected partnership. The abstractions chart the moods, doubts and challenges of experience; they evoke the forces of both inner terror and celestial bliss. The still lifes are symbols of nature's quieter pleasures, of social interaction and domestic intimacy. Alternately cosmic and homey in their subjects and effects, these two distinctive genres of image-making convey the extremes of human experience. We recognize their force and their invitation to reflect on Maxwell Smart's experience, and on our Canadian Jewish history.

Carol Zemel, Professor Emerita
Art History and Visual Culture
York University
2018

GLOSSARY

This glossary was researched, written and produced by the Azrieli Foundation's Holocaust Survivor Memoirs Program. For more information on their innovative educational programming and Holocaust survivor memoirs, visit https://memoirs.azrielifoundation.org/.

abstract expressionism A post–World War II art movement that emphasized an emotionally expressive, abstract and intuitive approach to artmaking. Prominent abstract expressionists include Jackson Pollock, Mark Rothko and Willem de Kooning.

Allied Zones of Germany and Austria The four zones that Germany and Austria were divided into after their defeat in World War II, each administered by one of the four major Allied powers — the United States, Britain, France and the Soviet Union. These administrative zones existed in Germany between 1945 and 1949, and in Austria between 1945 and 1955. In Austria, Vienna was divided into the four sectors and also held an International Sector. Austria regained its independence in 1955.

American Occupation Zone of Austria One of four zones in Austria created by the Allied occupying forces between 1945 and 1955. Geographically situated in Upper Austria (Oberösterreich), the American zone included the cities of Linz and Salzburg. Full administrative, military and political control was exercised by the United States in the American zone.

antisemitism Prejudice, discrimination, persecution or hatred against Jewish people, institutions, culture and symbols.

Bandera, Stepan (1909–1959) Ukrainian nationalist and leader of various nationalist groups, including a radical faction within the Organization of Ukrainian Nationalists (OUN), the OUN-B. Bandera saw the Nazis as allies and called for a "Ukrainian National Revolution" that would cleanse the Ukraine of its ethnic enemies: Poles, Soviets and Jews. His followers, known as Banderites (*Banderowcy*), were responsible for the massacre of tens of thousands of Jews and Poles during World War II. After Bandera declared an independent Ukrainian state in 1941, the Nazis placed him under house arrest and then deported him to Sachsenhausen concentration camp. After the war, Bandera continued to lead the OUN-B until he was assassinated by the KGB in 1959. In recent years, Bandera has gained popularity among Ukrainian nationalists as a symbol of freedom and independence. *See also Banderowcy.*

Banderowcy (Ukrainian; also Banderites) The informal term for Ukrainian nationalist guerillas led by Stepan Bandera under the auspices of the Organization of Ukrainian Nationalists (OUN) and its military wing, the Ukrainska Povstanska Armiya (UPA). Many of its members were antisemitic and led anti-Jewish violence and pogroms both during and after the war. Since the mid-1980s, Ukrainian right-wing nationalism has undergone a period of renewal in various forms — as the Congress of Ukrainian Nationalists political party; the Ukrainian National Assembly; and the Social-National Party of Ukraine (the Svoboda). *See also* Bandera, Stepan; Ukrainska Povstanska Armiya (UPA).

bar mitzvah (Hebrew; literally, one to whom commandments apply) The age of thirteen when, according to Jewish tradition, boys become religiously and morally responsible for their actions and are considered adults for the purpose of synagogue ritual. A bar mitzvah is also the synagogue ceremony and family celebration that mark the attainment of this status, during which the boy is called upon to read a portion of the Torah and recite the prescribed prayers in a public prayer forum.

black market An illegal and often informal economic system. After the war, many people risked participation in an underground black market to get ordinary goods and services, or informally bartered or traded within it.

Borduas, Paul-Émile (1905–1960) Famed Québécois artist who founded the Automatiste art movement in the 1940s and directed the publication of a manifesto titled *Refus global* in 1948. Both the movement and the manifesto were dedicated to expanding Quebec culture beyond the influences of past values. Borduas was eventually drawn to abstract expressionism and a textured style of painting. *See also* abstract expressionism; Riopelle, Jean-Paul.

British Mandate Palestine The area of the Middle East under British rule from 1923 to 1948, as established by the League of Nations after World War I. During that time, the United Kingdom severely restricted Jewish immigration. The Mandate area encompassed present-day Israel, Jordan, the West Bank and the Gaza Strip.

Canadian Jewish Congress (CJC) An advocacy organization and lobbying group for the Canadian Jewish community from 1919 to 2011. In 1947, the CJC convinced the Canadian government to re-issue Privy Council Order 1647 — originally adopted in 1942 to admit five hundred Jewish refugee children from Vichy France, although they never made it out — that allowed for one thousand Jewish children under the age of eighteen to be admitted to Canada. Under the auspices of the CJC, who would provide for the refugees' care, the War Orphans Project was established in April 1947 and the CJC began searching for Jewish war orphans with the help of the United Nations Relief and Rehabilitation Administration (UNRRA). Between 1947 and 1949, 1,123 young Jewish refugees came to Canada. The CJC was restructured in 2007 and its functions subsumed under the Centre for Israel and Jewish Affairs (CIJA) in 2011. *See also* United Nations Relief and Rehabilitation Administration.

chalutzim (Hebrew; pioneers) A term used within Zionist youth movements outside of Palestine to refer to its members who hoped to immigrate there.

cheder (Hebrew; literally, room) An Orthodox Jewish elementary school that teaches the fundamentals of Jewish religious observance and textual study, as well as the Hebrew language.

Chmielnicki, Bohdan (1595–1657; in Ukrainian, Khmelnytsky) A leader of the Cossacks, members of various ethnic groups in southern Russia, Ukraine and Siberia, who launched a series of military campaigns to free Ukraine from Polish domination and establish their own rule in the region. The Cossacks instigated a brutal uprising against the Jews by telling people that the Poles had sold them to the Jews as slaves. The Cossacks responded by slaughtering tens of thousands of Jews during 1648–1649 in what came to be known as the Chmielnicki Massacre. Historians estimate the death toll at about one hundred thousand, with the additional destruction of almost three hundred Jewish communities.

chuppah (Hebrew; literally, covering) The canopy used in traditional Jewish weddings that is usually made of a cloth (sometimes a prayer shawl) stretched or supported over four poles. It is meant to symbolize the home the couple will build together.

Cossacks *See* Chmielnicki, Bohdan.

Cyprus An island nation in the Mediterranean and former British colony that was granted independence from Great Britain in 1960. In the 1940s, Cyprus was the location of British detention camps for European Jewish refugees who were attempting to illegally immigrate to British Mandate Palestine. More than fifty thousand Jewish refugees were interned in these camps. *See also* British Mandate Palestine.

Displaced Persons (DP) camps Facilities set up by the Allied authorities and the United Nations Relief and Rehabilitation Administration (UNRRA) in October 1945 to resolve the refugee crisis that arose at the end of World War II. The camps provided temporary shelter and assistance to the millions of people — not only Jews — who had been displaced from their home countries as a result of the war and helped them prepare for resettlement. Approximately thirty thousand Jewish DPs entered Italy between September 1946 and June 1948. Italy, which eventually set up about twenty-five DP camps to house refugees, was the main transit point for Jews to reach British Mandate Palestine. *See also* United Nations Relief and Rehabilitation Administration (UNRRA).

Duplessis, Maurice (1890–1959) A conservative Canadian politician who formed a new nationalist party called Union Nationale and served five terms as premier of Quebec from 1936 to 1939 and from 1944 to 1959.

HaMotzi (Hebrew; who brings forth) The beginning of the blessing recited over bread before a meal.

Hayes, Saul (1906–1980) A Canadian lawyer and prominent advocate for the Canadian Jewish community. Hayes lobbied the Canadian government to relax their immigration restrictions during and after World War II. He served as executive director of the United Jewish Relief Agencies of Canada (UJRA) from 1938 to 1942 and executive director of the Canadian Jewish Congress (CJC) from 1940 to 1959. Among other honours, Hayes was made an officer of the Order of Canada in 1974 and continued to be involved with the CJC until his death. *See also* Canadian Jewish Congress.

Himmler, Heinrich (1900–1945) The most senior officer of the Nazi Party. Himmler oversaw the SS and the Gestapo and, as administrator of the Third Reich, was directly responsible for implementing the "Final Solution" — the mass murder of the European Jewish population. Himmler established the Nazi concentration camp system in which millions of Jews, Roma and others considered "undesirable" under Nazi racial policies were either murdered or kept imprisoned under brutal conditions. Himmler committed suicide on May 23, 1945.

Jewish Brigade A battalion that was formed in September 1944 under the command of the British Eighth Army. The Jewish Brigade included more than five thousand volunteers from Palestine. After the war, the Brigade was essential in helping Jewish refugees and organizing their entry into Palestine. It was disbanded by the British in 1946.

Judenrat (German; pl. Judenräte) Jewish Council. A group of Jewish leaders appointed by the Germans to administer and provide services to the local Jewish population under occupation and carry out Nazi orders. The Judenräte, which appeared to be self-governing entities but were actually under complete Nazi control, faced difficult and complex moral decisions under brutal conditions and remain a contentious subject. The chairmen had to decide whether to comply or refuse to comply with Nazi demands. Some were killed by the Nazis for refusing, while others committed suicide. Jewish officials who advocated compliance thought that cooperation might save at least some of the population. Some who denounced resistance efforts did so because they believed that armed resistance would bring death to the entire community.

Kandinsky, Wassily (1866–1944) A Russian-born artist known for his early adoption of the abstract style of painting, a style that he believed could express the creator's emotions and universal spiritual ideas.

Kielce pogrom The July 1946 riots in a city in Poland where about two hundred fifty Jews lived after the war (the pre-war Jewish population had been more than twenty thousand. After the false report of a young Polish boy being kidnapped by Jews, police arrested and beat Jewish residents in the city, inciting a mob of hundreds of Polish civilians to violently attack and kill forty Jews while police stood by. Combined with other post-war antisemitic incidents throughout Poland — other pogroms occurred in Rzeszów, Krakow, Tarnów and Sosnowiec, and robberies and blackmail were common — this event was the catalyst for a mass exodus; between July 1945 and September 1946, more than eighty thousand Jews left Poland.

Molotov-Ribbentrop Pact (also known as the Treaty of Non-Aggression between Germany and the USSR) The treaty that was signed on August 24, 1939, and was colloquially known as the Molotov-Ribbentrop pact, after signatories Soviet foreign minister Vyacheslav Molotov and German foreign minister Joachim von Ribbentrop. The main provisions of the pact stipulated that the two countries would not go to war with each other and that they would both remain neutral if either one was attacked by a third party. One of the key components of the treaty was the division of various independent countries — including Poland — into Nazi and Soviet spheres of influence and areas of occupation. The Nazis breached the pact by launching a major offensive against the Soviet Union on June 22, 1941.

Orthodox Judaism The set of beliefs and practices of Jews for whom the observance of Jewish law is closely connected to faith; it is characterized by strict religious observance of Jewish dietary laws, restrictions on work on the Sabbath and holidays, and a code of modesty in dress.

Passover One of the major festivals of the Jewish calendar, Passover takes place over eight days in the spring. One of the main observances of the holiday is to recount the story of Exodus, the Jews' flight from slavery in Egypt, at a ritual meal called a seder. The name itself refers to the fact that God "passed over" the houses of the Jews when he set about slaying the firstborn sons of Egypt as the last of the ten plagues aimed at convincing Pharaoh to free the Jews.

Petliura, Symon (1879–1926) A journalist and politician who advocated for an independent Ukraine. Petliura fought against both Bolshevik and White Russian forces in Ukraine and, after World War I, briefly led the Ukrainian government until the country came under Soviet control. In 1924, Petliura settled in Paris, where, two years later, he was assassinated by a Jewish anarchist, exacerbating Ukrainian nationalist antisemitism. His legacy is controversial due to the Ukrainian army's pogroms against Jews during his time as leader, when an estimated thirty-five thousand to fifty thousand Jews were killed.

pogrom (Russian; to wreak havoc, to demolish) A violent attack on a distinct ethnic group. The term most commonly refers to nineteenth- and twentieth-century attacks on Jews in the Russian Empire. *See also* Kielce pogrom.

Pollock, Jackson (1912–1956) A famous American abstract expressionist artist best known for his drip paintings, a new, original style of work he created in the 1940s. *See also* abstract expressionism.

Righteous Among the Nations A title bestowed by Yad Vashem, the Holocaust Martyrs' and Heroes' Remembrance Authority in Jerusalem, to honour non-Jews who risked their lives to help save Jews during the Holocaust. A commission was established in 1963 to award the title. If a person fits certain criteria and the story is carefully corroborated, the honouree is awarded with a medal and a certificate and commemorated on the Wall of Honour at the Garden of the Righteous in Jerusalem.

Ringelblum, Emanuel (1900–1944) The historian, educator, relief worker and writer who is most known for his diligence and leadership in archiving testimonials and other material evidence from the Warsaw ghetto. Ringelblum's organization and its archive, called Oneg Shabbat, clandestinely documented the ongoing strife, daily life and persecution in the Warsaw ghetto. Members of Oneg Shabbat buried the collection of materials in a number of large milk jugs and metal containers, two of which were discovered after the war. The more than twenty-five thousand pages are held at the Jewish Historical Institute in Warsaw.

Riopelle, Jean-Paul (1923–2002) An internationally renowned Québécois painter and sculptor who was closely aligned with the Automatiste movement. Riopelle, a student of Paul-Émile Borduas, was also a primary contributor to the *Refus global* manifesto. His large body of work, which is represented in museums worldwide, has been described as spontaneous and layered and has been lauded for its use of colour and original techniques. *See also* Borduas, Paul-Émile.

Sabbath (in Hebrew, Shabbat; in Yiddish, Shabbes, Shabbos) The weekly day of rest beginning Friday at sunset and ending Saturday at nightfall, ushered in by the lighting of candles on Friday evening and the recitation of blessings over wine and challah (egg bread). A day of celebration as well as prayer. It is customary to eat three festive meals, attend synagogue services and refrain from doing any work or travelling.

Sich A Ukrainian nationalist militia that operated in Buczacz, Poland, in early July 1941, after Germany invaded the Soviet Union. The Sich, named after a legion of riflemen in World War I, arrested and killed retreating Soviet soldiers as well as a number of local Jews. The Sich operated for several weeks prior to German control over the region, targeting Jews for forced labour and perpetrating various acts of violence against both Jews and Poles. After the Germans occupied Buczacz, many Sich members became local policemen and, allied with the Nazis, continued to target Jews. *See also* Ukrainska Povstanska Armiya (UPA).

Star of David (in Hebrew, *Magen David*) The six-pointed star that is the ancient and most recognizable symbol of Judaism. During World War II, Jews in Nazi-occupied areas were frequently forced to wear a badge or armband with the Star of David on it as an identifying mark of their lesser status and to single them out as targets for persecution.

tallis (Yiddish; in Hebrew, *tallit*) Prayer shawl. A four-cornered ritual garment traditionally worn by adult Jewish men during morning prayers and on the Day of Atonement (Yom Kippur). One usually wears the *tallis* over one's shoulders but some choose to place it over their heads to express awe in the presence of God.

Torah (Hebrew) The Five Books of Moses (the first five books of the Bible), also called the Pentateuch. The Torah is the core of Jewish scripture, traditionally believed to have been given to Moses on Mount Sinai. In Christianity it is referred to as the "Old Testament."

Ukrainian Auxiliary Police (in German, Ukrainische Hilfspolizei) A force formed in the wake of the German occupation of eastern Poland and the Ukraine in June 1941. The Ukrainian Auxiliary Police actively collaborated with the Nazis in the implementation of their plans to persecute and eventually mass murder Jews. They escorted Jews to forced labour sites, guarded the ghettos and engaged in mass-murder shooting operations.

Ukrainska Povstanska Armiya (UPA) A Ukrainian insurgent army connected to the Organization of Ukrainian Nationalists (OUN). Led by nationalist ideology to create an independent Ukraine, the UPA — anti-Soviet and anti-Polish, with antisemitic elements as well — targeted various civilians and soldiers between 1942 and 1945, killing tens of thousands of Jews and Poles. The UPA was formally disbanded in 1949 but continued to have a localized presence until 1956. *See also Banderowcy.*

United Nations Relief and Rehabilitation Administration (UNRRA) An international relief agency created at a forty-four nation conference in Washington, DC, on November 9, 1943, to provide economic assistance and basic necessities to war refugees. It was especially active in repatriating and assisting refugees in the formerly Nazi-occupied European nations immediately after World War II.

Workmen's Circle (in Yiddish, Der Arbeter Ring) An organization founded in New York in 1892 that was closely tied to the socialist labour movement and secular Yiddish culture. A branch of the Workmen's Circle opened in Montreal in 1907 and offered its nearly 1,000 members various educational and social opportunities as well as health benefits. Now renamed as the Worker's Circle, the organization continues to exist in Montreal.

PHOTOGRAPHS

The only document Maxwell has that shows his birth name, Oziac Fromm (Ozic From). This certificate was administered under the direction of the security police as part of the foreign-control service of Bucharest, Romania. It identifies Maxwell (then Oziac) as a Jewish Polish immigrant and indicates that he is enrolled for immigration to Palestine by the Red Cross Society and is allowed to temporarily reside in Bucharest. Issued December 20, 1945, in Bucharest, Romania.

Maxwell (top left) on the train from Italy to Bremen, Germany, from where he boarded a ship to Canada. 1948.

193

The first photo of Maxwell taken in Canada. Montreal, April 18, 1949.

Maxwell and Helen's wedding day. From left to right: Helen's father, Srewl (Issie) Safran; Helen; Maxwell; Helen's mother, Masha Safran; and Helen's sister, Rhoda. Montreal, December 1950.

Maxwell and Helen with their daughter, Faigie (Faith). Montreal, 1958.

Faigie and Lorne, Maxwell and Helen's children. Montreal, 1960.

Maxwell's first reunion with his aunt Erna and uncle Jacob after the war. From left to right: Maxwell; his daughter, Faith; his aunt Erna (née Kissel) Klanfer; his son, Lorne; and his uncle, Jacob Klanfer. Tel Aviv, Israel, circa 1964.

Jacob and Erna Klanfer. Tel Aviv, Israel, 1960s.

Maxwell praying at the Wailing Wall. Jerusalem, Israel, circa 1964.

The gravestones of Maxwell's aunt Erna and uncle Jacob. The stone on the left reads: Orna [Erna] Klanfer. Daughter of Rachel and Moshe. Passed July 11, 1988. The stone on the right reads: Yaakov [Jacob] Klanfer. Son of Shalom Z"L. Passed December 18, 1976. Located outside Tel Aviv, Israel, this is the only place Maxwell knows that he has family. 2007.

Maxwell and Helen Safran Smart. Montreal, circa 1980.

Helen beside the sterling silver candelabrum that was given to Maxwell by his aunt, Erna. The candelabrum belonged to Maxwell's mother — it was given to her on her wedding day by Maxwell's grandfather — and is Maxwell's only remaining connection to his home in Buczacz, Poland. Montreal, date unknown.

Maxwell in front of his painting *Autumn Rain #1*, oil on canvas, 48 × 36 in., 1984. Montreal, circa 1985.

Maxwell and Tina on their wedding day. Montreal, September 1994.

Maxwell's daughter, Faith, with his granddaughter Tara, age two, and his son
Anthony, age seven, at Maxwell's studio. Montreal, 1990s.

Maxwell's in-laws, Masha and Issie Safran, with two of his grandchildren, Brandon
and Tara, on Passover. Montreal, 1997.

Maxwell's friend and business associ-
ate, Eddie Stern, with his wife, Shirley.
Montreal, date unknown. Photo
credit: The Stern family.

Tina and Maxwell (seated) with Tina's
brothers and sisters-in-law. From left
to right: Angelo and Nina Russo; Mary
and Tony Russo. (Montreal, 1990s.)

Maxwell (centre) with his two good friends and fellow Holocaust survivors
Thomas O. Hecht (left) and David Azrieli (right). Both Thomas and David wrote
their memoirs — published, respectively, as *Czech Mate* (2007) and *One Step
Ahead* (2001) — and encouraged Maxwell to write his story. Montreal, circa 2010.

Maxwell at work in his studio. Montreal, circa 2000.

View of Maxwell's work in his Galerie d'Art Maxwell. Montreal, 2018. Photo credit: Ryan Blau PBL Photography

Heaven and Music #1, oil on canvas, 18 × 24 in., 1963.

Maxwell's family at the opening of Galerie d'Art Maxwell. Back row, from left to right: his daughter-in-law, Sharon; his son Lorne; his son Anthony; Maxwell; Tina; his son-in-law, Ian; and his daughter, Faith. In front: his grandsons Brandon (left) and Adam (right). Photo credit: Joe Donohue

Clockwise from top: Maxwell's son-in-law, Ian; his grandson Jay; his daughter, Faith; and his granddaughter, Tara.

Tina and her son, Anthony. Montreal, 2008.

Maxwell together with Janek's family in Israel. Janek's auntie, Jehudith Shifris, also a Holocaust survivor, is seated by her husband, Shimon. Standing from left to right, Maxwell with Janek's cousins, Miri Gershoni and her brother Pinchus Shifris, 2019.

Maxwell reunited with Tova Barkai, whom he and Janek saved during World War II when she was two years old. From left to right: Tova's son Ofer Barkai, Maxwell, Tova Barkai, Tova's granddaughters Maia and Lital, and Ofer's wife, Miri, 2019.

Canada Yad Vashem

The Government of Canada
is honoured to present this certificate of recognition to

Max Smart

a Holocaust Survivor

on April 23, 2013
to pay tribute to your profound courage, strength, and dignity.

During Canada's chair year of the International Holocaust Remembrance Alliance, the Government of Canada will work with community partners to preserve survivor testimony as an invaluable resource for Holocaust education.

Few can fully understand the unimaginable suffering, cruelty, and loss that you witnessed and endured. Your remarkable story serves as a compelling reminder to all humankind of our obligation to learn from the past.

By sharing your story, you strengthen the Canadian Society for Yad Vashem's mission of ensuring that the universal lessons of the Shoah are never forgotten.

Your passing of the torch of remembrance encourages future generations to be vigilant against all forms of hatred and intolerance and to embrace inclusiveness and pluralism.

Jason Kenney
MINISTER OF CITIZENSHIP,
IMMIGRATION AND MULTICULTURALISM

Mark Adler
MEMBER OF PARLIAMENT

Fran Sonshine
NATIONAL CHAIR OF THE
CANADIAN SOCIETY FOR YAD VASHEM

A certificate issued by Yad Vashem and the government of Canada recognizing Maxwell's achievements and his contributions to Canadian society.

Maxwell in front of his painting *Downtown* (oil on canvas, 84 × 48 in., 2017).

INDEX

Maxwell Smart's name has been abbreviated to "Max."
Page numbers in italics refer to illustrations.